THE SHOTOKAN DAWN SUPPLEMENT

THE SHOTOKAN DAWN
SUPPLEMENT

DR. CLIVE LAYTON

MONA BOOKS UK

55 Bridge Street, Llangefni, Anglesey, North Wales, LL77 7PN, Great Britain

First Published in 2007
by
MONA BOOKS UK
55 Bridge Street, Llangefni, Anglesey, North Wales, LL77 7PN, Great Britain
Tel: +44 (0)1248 723486
www.monabooks.co.uk
email: mike@monabooks.co.uk

The moral right of the author has been asserted.

First Edition

British Library Cataloguing-in-Publication Data.
A catalogue record for this book is available from the British Library.

ISBN 978 0 9555122 2 3

DEDICATION

TO

RACHEL, PANDORA & CEDAR

for being patient

AND

TO

VERNON BELL

who died whilst this book was in production

ACKNOWLEDGEMENTS

The author is grateful to the following people for their help during the preparation of *The Shotokan Dawn Supplement*: Rachel Layton; Pandora Layton; Vernon Bell, 10th Dan, Chief Instructor to Tenshin-Shinyo-Ryu Jujitsu (European Jujitsu Union), 3rd Dan Judo, 3rd Dan Karate-do; Harry Cook, 7th Dan, Chief Instructor to the Seijinkai Karate-Do Association; John Morgan, 6th Dan, Goshin-jutsu; Gordon Thompson, 3rd Dan; Nicholas Adamou, 8th Dan, Chief Instructor to the International Shotokan Karate Association.

Photo Credits: Nicholas Adamou: 135; Clive Layton: 138, 139; Rachel Layton: 171; Mona Books (UK): ix, 16, 18, 19, 21, 26, 29, 30, 31, 32, 33, 35, 37, 38, 39, 41, 46, 47, 48, 51, 53, 55, 58, 59, 68, 74, 78, 79, 90, 96, 111, 114, 118, 120, 122, 136; Gordon Thompson (copies of these photographs are available from the Budoshin Company, 32 Peel Close, Heslington, York, YO1 5EN, England): 50, 60, 61, 66, 67, 86, 87, 88, 101.

Publisher's Appeal: The publisher of this work has been unable to trace or contact a number of owners (original photographer or other) of photographs used in this book. Such uncredited persons will be duly acknowledged by the publisher in any future edition of this book upon notification of proof of entitlement.

Front cover: Master Murakami in the process of delivering a *right yoko-tobi-geri* upon Reg Armstrong, on the lawn tennis court of 12, Maybush Road, Hornchurch, Essex (July, 1959). Taken from *Shotokan Dawn: Vol. I* (p. 165).

Back cover: Bell leads *jodan-age-empi-uchi* practice at the Wheatsheaf *dojo*, Kenton Street, London, WC1 (1958).

CONTENTS

FOREWORD

*S*hotokan Dawn is truly a brilliant work. Every *karateka* I have spoken to agrees that Dr. Layton has created a masterpiece, encapsulating not only the facts of those first ten years of Shotokan in Great Britain, but also the spirit of that early training. How he achieved this I know not – though one suspects a love of the art, a lot of hard work, and genuine writing talent. Of one thing I am confident, *Shotokan Dawn* will endure.

Knowing Dr. Layton's eye for detail and wishing to leave no stone unturned in recording the history of Shotokan in Britain, I was not surprised when he informed me that he was going to write a supplement to *Shotokan Dawn* once additional material had become available. Such devotion is to be applauded.

I have read *The Shotokan Dawn Supplement* and can recommend it without reservation. It is essential reading for all who want to understand the development of their art in Great Britain.

Vernon Bell – founder of the British Karate movement
November, 2002

PREFACE

When the two-volume, *Shotokan Dawn: A Selected, Early History of Shotokan Karate in Great Britain (1956-1966)* was being printed, Vernon Bell, the founder of British karate, discovered, unbelievably, a box containing lost files and two BKF registers after more than seven years searching. These files and registers contain both important information, such as membership forms and correspondence from 'lost' clubs, and miscellaneous material covering the period in question. It was felt that in order to make *Shotokan Dawn* as complete as possible, a supplement was in order, using the original work as a reference point through which additional material could be inserted. Thus, information in this book is available for insertion by volume, page and line/paragraph to the original. When a line is given and new material is to be inserted, on many occasions a new paragraph is required. The author does not indicate new paragraphs. Whilst the majority of information is suitable for insertion, some is in the form of annotation, though no distinction is made between the two here. The reader may well have already read *Shotokan Dawn,* in which case insertion of the new material will be in light of prior knowledge, though if the reader has not previously read *Shotokan Dawn*, it may, of course, be read in unison with 'The Supplement,' inserting the additions and annotations as and when they appear.

In the Preface to *Shotokan Dawn*, it was noted that, 'a substantial amount [of material] has been lost.' Now, with the uncovering of other files and a document entitled, *Schedule and Inventory of All British Karate Federation Property, Equipment and Documents as at the 17th September 1964*, we have a much clearer idea of what has not survived. The author is pleased to announce that all the relevant material kept by Bell, and deemed relevant by the author, has now been integrated into the three books, at least up to the 17th September 1964, assuming that files have not been pillaged or some of their contents lost. Many of Bell's reply letters may never have been kept, and a simple handwritten note on a letter giving a reply date is provided in many cases. The *Schedule ...* is a fascinating document, and its content is reproduced in its entirety as an appendix.

The Shotokan Dawn Supplement also contains five additional forms of information. Firstly, much of the content of *Shotokan Dawn* was based on photocopies of original documents. With long-term access to the originals, it was evident that a few documents, often an odd reverse side, had escaped being photocopied, and the details contained therein had, therefore, been excluded in the previous work. Secondly, drawing exclusively from original documents, this supplement has allowed the author, with hindsight, to elaborate on one or two issues that he now regards as historically important given newly discovered information. Thirdly, a few contributors to the original found, not surprisingly perhaps, that on reading the books, memories, long forgotten, had been rekindled, and at the author's request, Vernon Bell, Gordon Thompson and Nicholas Adamou have added to their original contributions with further reminiscences. Fourthly, a good number of additional, contemporaneous photographs, known to have existed but believed lost, have also been unearthed, and many of these have been included, as have recent photographs of old *dojos*. These photographs have been inserted at locations that either relate to new information, or as they relate to page number in *Shotokan Dawn*. In the latter case, the volume and page number where the photograph should be inserted, is given (e.g. I/100) after the caption. Fifthly, thirteen appendices, most displaying tables and graphs of BKF information are also provided. The author is particularly pleased with the tables and graphs, based, as they are, on the records of one thousand one hundred and eighty BKF members (Part 1), with an additional thirty-four members added to include BKF students in Ireland (Part 2). Readers are directed to, *A Selected, Early History of Shotokan Karate in Ireland (1960 -1964)*, to gain the full picture of BKF involvement in Eire. It will be appreciated that such tables and graphs are not always based on the same figures, as some membership forms are incomplete. 83.4% of the ages of BKF students are known at the time of their application, for example, compared to 85.3% of data relating to social class.

As noted in the Preface of *Shotokan Dawn*, and the author would like to reiterate the point here, if there are errors, and of course everything possible has been done to minimise such errors, then the author apologises in advance. It has only been possible to work with the material that has survived, or that the author has been privy to, and any errors are made in good faith. Errors detected to date are almost exclusively related to Bell's handwriting, which can be extremely difficult to read, and this has caused a few problems with some surnames. These surnames are corrected here. Also, once again, and with Bell's permission, it was felt that his penchant for overly long sentences at times had to be corrected to aid reader comfort; similarly, occasionally, incorrect grammar has been corrected.

The manner in which this book has been written with regard to the insertion of new information reveals to the reader, very effectively as it so happens, how *Shotokan Dawn* was constructed – piece-by-piece, like a jigsaw.

What is here today will be gone tomorrow, so the maxim has been to record whilst the sun shines, as it were. Clearly, Clio, the Greek Muse of History, hadn't finished with me as I thought she had. With the publication of the one hundred and fifty-seven thousand word *Shotokan Dawn,* what had previously been regarded as the Dark Ages of British Shotokan became brightly illuminated. With the publication of the additional forty-nine thousand words contained in *The Shotokan Dawn Supplement,* our knowledge of Shotokan's past has increased by thirty-one per cent, and so the illumination has become noticeably brighter still.

January, 2007

CLIVE LAYTON, M.A., Ph.D (Lond), 7th Dan.

THE SHOTOKAN DAWN SUPPLEMENT

PART 1

ADDITIONS TO VOL. I OF *SHOTOKAN DAWN*

Page 17, line 2 – Confirmation of Bell's birth: General Register Office {births} – December 1922, Romford, Vol. 4a, p. 855.

line 3 – Leonard Bell was born in 1895 (General Register Office {births}: June 1895, Edmonton, Vol. 3a, p. 483).

line 4 – Elsie Sapsworth was born on the 1st July 1897 (General Register Office {births}: September 1897, Edmonton, Vol. 3a, p. 507).

line 11 – Leonard Bell's death (General Register Office {deaths}, March 1976, Colchester, Vol. 9, p. 2730).

line 12 – Elsie Bell's death (General Register Office {deaths}, September 1977, Colchester, Vol. 9, p. 1883).

line 14 – Frederick Augustus Bell was born in 1854/55 in Waltham Abbey, Essex. Marrying in 1888 (General Register Office {marriages}, September 1888, Edmonton, Vol. 3a, page 376), he and his wife, Eliza Anne (born 1867/68), from Riseley, Bedfordshire, had at least four children: Percy, Douglas, Leonard and Lillian. According to the 1901 Census, Frederick was a clerk. Presumably, Vernon Bell's notion that his grandfather had invented the photographic enlarger is likely to have been passed down in the family, but its veracity is yet to be determined. In 1901, the Bell family were sufficiently well off to have a servant, named Louisa.

line 14 – Elsie Sapsworth was the second of at least five children to Arthur John Sapsworth (General Register Office {births}: December 1865, Edmonton, Vol. 3a, p. 198). He married in 1889 (General Register Office {marriages}, December 1889, Edmonton, Vol. 3a, page 474), and he and his wife, Hilda's (born 1866/67) known children in 1901 were: Constance, Elsie, Hilda and Miriam. According to the 1901 Census, Arthur Sapsworth was a mechanical engineer. The 1881 Census tells us that Arthur Sapsworth's father – a labourer born in Hatfield, Hertfordshire, in 1821/22 – and his mother (born 1832/33,

Wilfred Sapsworth – and, underneath, Bell's handwriting (I/22)

in Cheshunt, Hertfordshire), were William and Jane, respectively.

Page 22, line 10 – Wilfred Frank Sapsworth was a younger brother to Elsie (General Register Office {births}: September 1903, Edmonton, Vol. 3a, p. 680).

Page 25, line 14 – Bell married Rita Wendy Meeson on the 27th August 1942 at the Register Office, Edmonton. Meeson lived in Southgate and was twenty years of age at the time. Her father, John, was a company director. On the marriage certificate, under 'Rank or Profession' Bell's details are given as follows: 'Cadet, No. 1586946. Royal Airforce (bank clerk).'
    line 15 – the date should read '1942' (General Register Office {marriages}: September 1942, Edmonton, Vol. 3a, p. 2749).
    line 16 – The twin boys were named Ivan C. R. and Warwick D. F. (General Register Office {births}: September 1945, Stepney, Vol. 1c, p. 68). They later emigrated to Australia with their mother. Rita died in the early 1990s, and Warwick died following a road accident in New Zealand.

Page 26, 2nd paragraph – On Wednesday, 7th December 1949, the *Romford Times* carried a clip under 'Entertainments' entitled, 'Gaumont Judo Show.' It read: 'Tokyo Joe, this week's attraction at Gaumont, Romford, is a melodrama set in post-war Japan. Japan and ju-jutsu are synonymous – so, naturally, the art of self-defence is to be seen on the screen in this film. But Gaumont management thought filmgoers would like to see ju-jutsu practised in the fourth dimension. So, on Friday at 8.30 p.m., Vernon Bell and his associates will enact an exciting scene from the film on [the] Gaumont stage.' Following the display, another clip, *Getting Tough at the Gaumont*, presumably from the same paper, but undated, read: 'Filmgoers at the Gaumont, Romford, on Friday, saw not only the tough scenes in which Humphrey Bogart takes a few tumbles in Japan, the home of ju-jutsu, in the film, Tokyo Joe, but an able demonstration of ju-jutsu on the stage. This was in the form of a playet demonstrating the art, and one of the performers, a 19-year-old girl, was applauded for the ease in which she threw her burly male antagonists to the floor. The show was under the leadership of Mr. Vernon Bell, the physical culture [*sic*].'

Page 34, line 27 – 'Musu' should be spelt 'Muso,' and 'Jujutsu' should be spelt 'Jojutsu.'

Taken at the Plaza Cinema, Romford, just before the *Tokyo Joe* demonstration in 1949 – left to right, back row: David Anderson (Bell's assistant judo instructor in the early 1950s and a builder by trade), unknown, W. Pitt (bus driver); middle row – Leonard Botterell (carpenter), Alan Clements (painter), Charles Steggles, Robert Cavender (post office worker, and Bell's chief judo assistant); front row – Bell, Lucy (at 14 yrs), John Ritchie. The badge is of the Bell School of Judo (I/26).

Vernon Bell directs two judo students, one of whom has just performed *harai-goshi* (sweeping loin throw) – Mayfield Secondary Boys School, Ilford, *c.* 1955 (I/30).

Page 36, line 20 – remove 'sixteenth' and insert 'ninety-sixth.'
    line 32 – *Vaincre ou Mourir: Karate-Do*, was published in 1955.

Page 40, line 8 – The fact that Hiroo Mochizuki trained in Shotokan comes, in part, from an article, *The Classical Path of Yoseikan Ryu*, by James Shortt, that appeared in *International Budo* magazine (October 1978, pp. 15-17). Shortt noted that: 'At the age of fifteen Mochizuki Hiroo joined the Shotokan karate school of Gichin Funakoshi and for three years studied the techniques of Shotokan.' Mochizuki was fifteen in 1951-52. Where he studied and graded is unclear.
    line 8 – Seydell received his *Shodan* in 1959, and formed the Deutsche Karate-Bund (German Karate Federation) on the 29th July, 1961. The DKB joined the European Karate Federation on the 2nd December that same year. So, Bell's recollection that they took their *Shodans* together, is incorrect, though they did meet in 1957 (almost certainly for the first time, on October 25th/26th).
    line 9 – Cherix opened the first Swiss karate *dojo* in Sion, apparently in 1957.

Page 42, photographs – The dates on both photographs are more likely to read, '1957.'

Page 43, line 5 – In a translation of a later undated article in *Budo-Presse*, entitled, 'The Founder of European Karate-Do: Official Interview with Monsieur Henri Plee, 3rd Dan – The Coming of the Japanese Masters,' Plee makes some comments on Hiroo Mochizuki: 'He taught us the *kiai*. He was not only kind, he was also technically very good ... I found him extraordinary, very good and beautiful [of movement].'

Page 50, line 8 – In a translation of a later, undated article in *Budo-Presse,* entitled, 'The Founder of European Karate-Do: Official Interview with Monsieur Henri Plee, 3rd Dan – The Coming of the Japanese Masters,' Plee notes that Hiyugo became mentally ill.

Page 51, line 19 – According to Plee, these experts were both 2nd Dan, but reference is also made to a 4th Dan.

Page 52, line 6 – To confuse matters, in a letter to Plee dated the 21st February 1957, which pre-dates Plee's signing of Bell's licence, Bell wrote: 'I would like you to mark and sign, and authorise, my black belt *Shodan* karate grade, and return it to me when you reply.'

Page 54, line 7 – The Japanese expert was Kaoru Mishiku.

Page 55, line 24 – *The Practical Manual* ... was written by Lasserre.

Page 56, line 15 – In this letter, Bell reported that: 'At my recent visit to Mr. K. Abbe's *dojo*, I was informed by his chief instructor, Mr. Wood (3rd Dan), during our conversation, which developed around karate, that the London Judo Society (second largest club in England) was shortly expecting the arrival of two Japanese karate experts.' These experts never arrived.

Page 58, line 26 – In a letter to Jurgen Seydel dated the 23rd April 1958, Bell wrote that 'from our old original members on the first course, we have only have three left out of the one dozen who started eighteen months ago.' If this is accurate therefore, Bell began teaching karate in Hornchurch in October 1956. In fact, Bell may well have begun teaching as much as two months earlier. The fourth column,

FÉDÉRATION FRANÇAISE DE KARATÉ

34, RUE DE LA MONTAGNE-SAINTE-GENEVIÈVE - PARIS-Vᵉ

KARATE CLUB DE FRANCE

LICENCE N° 000521

M r V.C.F BELL

Adresse 137 Hillview Ave. HORNCHURCH
Essex

Le Président Fédéral,	Le Président, du Club,	Le Titulaire,

G R A D E

COULEUR DE LA CEINTURE	DATE d'obtention	SIGNATURES DES EXAMINATEURS
4ᵉ DAN Noire		
3ᵉ DAN Noire		
2ᵉ DAN Noire		
1ᵉʳ DAN Noire	13/3/57	
1ᵉʳ KYU Marron		
2ᵉ KYU Marron		
3ᵉ KYU Marron		
4ᵉ KYU Blanche		
5ᵉ KYU Blanche		
6ᵉ KYU Blanche		

Vignettes annuelles et Assurances M.N.S.

Bell's FFK licence showing his *Shodan* grading date signed by Plee (I/52)

'Grade' (appearing before 'New Grade' and 'Date of Grading'), of the BKF grading register, appears to record the date entry of karate training with Bell. If these dates are to be relied upon, then the earliest date is the 18th August 1956, when D. Clarke was entered. This was followed by D. Blake, P. Byron, and G. Tucker, all of whom are entered for 16th September 1956. The remaining entry for 1956 is M. Manning, who is recorded as the 23rd September. These students may have completed a judo or jujitsu application form, but it does seem strange to include them in a karate register if they were not practising the art. To highlight this point further, both Tucker and Manning completed Bell's jujitsu application form on the 2nd June 1956, yet they was required to complete a further, different jujitsu form three months later, on the 16th and 23rd September, respectively, when they were entered in the BKF Register. Similarly, Guilfoyle is entered in the register as 3rd January 1957, yet his application form shows that he signed his enrolment forms to study judo with Bell on the 2nd January 1956, and payment made the following day. Bell could have inserted 1957 instead of 1956, making Guilfoyle the first recorded karate student (after Bell, of course) in Britain. On the other hand, which is the more likely, it could simply indicate that an annual subscription was due, but this begs the question as to whether he was training on his existing subscription. Elliott is entered in the BKF grading register on the 1st April 1957, when he enrolled with Bell, initially for jujitsu, at least as early as before the 15th May 1954. Maybe he predates all other BKF students – who knows? Throughout 1957 (that is, in the three forms to have survived – Miles, Pearson and Anderson), Bell was still using his jujitsu application form for BKF students, though the word 'jujitsu' was sometimes crossed out and 'karate' inserted in its place. All this is highly suggestive that the BKF grading register is recording something other than jujitsu or judo, and one may claim within acceptable confidence limits that the BKF grading register is recording the first BKF students.

Page 60, line 13 – Tucker's resignation of the 21st July 1958 was temporary, though indefinite. A year and a half later, Bell wrote to Tucker (letter lost) at Crewkerne School, and Tucker replied on the 10th January 1960. Tucker noted that: 'I am still very tied down and can find no way of practising karate. I think, therefore, it would be best if I resign completely from karate.' Bell had sent Tucker some newspaper clippings, and Tucker refers to one unknown clipping, so: 'I see from one of the papers that there is now a rival karate club in

London. I believe it was featured in the *People*. How does this tie-up with your licence from the Yoseikan? I thought our club was the only one permitted.' Of course, the London club may have been a reference to the Wheatsheaf, which wasn't in existence when Tucker left. If it refers to a genuine 'rival,' the author is unaware of such a club.

     line 19 – According to Bell, Clarke was involved in the printing trade.

Page 65, line 31 – A previously unknown letter, of which two copies exist, dated the 20th June 1957 and 22nd June 1957, and addressed to 'The Editor' of, no doubt, a number of newspapers, is extremely important, given its early date and contents. Bell introduces himself and the art of karate to the media for the first time. As the letter is so important, it will be reproduced in its entirety. Bell wrote: 'I wish to draw your attention to the following information, which I feel may be of considerable interest and news to your readers, as being of a rare and unusual nature, and which you may find sufficiently interesting to wish to approach us for further information.

'The news is, that for the first time ever in Great Britain, the true deadly Japanese art of combat, i.e. karate, has recently … commenced practice as it is done in Japan, and an official written charter has been granted to myself by the French Karate Federation (which is the European official controlling body and representative of the Japanese Karate Federation – the Yoseikan) to establish the true karate in Gt. Britain, and to establish, promote, organise and control the British Karate Federation, which has now been formulated to control, strictly and correctly, karate in Great Britain, under the statues and auspices of the FFK and Yoseikan in Japan.

'Regarding myself, I am the first Englishman, as far as records show, ever to gain an authentic recognised black belt in karate, and it was my proud privilege to visit FFK in Paris in April of this year to be graded in karate and to receive my official diploma of the Yoseikan from the president of the FFK (who graded me) who, himself, is the founder and leading exponent of karate in Europe. During my visit to the FFK in Paris, I practised with, contested, and had competitions with, the leading French black belt karate experts (all Japanese trained) including French experts and champions in 'le Savette' and French Boxing, giving a good account of myself. I also received whilst over there, the official charter to establish karate in Gt. Britain – in the jurisdiction of the BKF, which is the only true authentic karate controlling body in this country.

'In the last few months I have been privileged to have in training under me about ten keen practising students of karate, of whom several have in this week been graded to their first grade in karate – that of white belt. These men, besides myself, are the first ever to achieve a grade in this country in the deadly and dangerous karate, and as these students of mine are all local and Essex men, I feel it is a distinction and an honour for them to be the pioneers of a new and highly skilled art in England.

'Shortly, in July, we have arranged with the FFK to send over one of their leading karate experts to take a week-end course in karate in this area, in the person of Mr. Hoang Nam, champion karateist of Indo-China, who will be arriving on July 6th. Also, in November, a team of four leading continental experts are coming to England to give large public displays in karate and Karate-Do, on which occasion will be the official opening of the International Karate Federation and the European Karate Union, to which our British Federation is affiliated. Our karate federation students meet at present for instruction and practice, under myself, at the above address [12, Maybush Rd] at week-ends, and you are cordially invited to attend with your reporter and official photographer to witness and report on the art.

'If you care to write [to] me or telephone (any day 12 noon to 1p.m.) to fix an appointment to visit us at a very early date, then I shall be very happy to accommodate you. On July 6th we expect to give the first ever karate display at the Epping Police Fair, which you are welcome to cover, and we invite you to attend at a fixed time during our week-end course, July 6th & July 7th, to report and take pictures. It is hoped that our federation will shortly establish itself in permanent headquarters in London, with official practice time.

'I would be obliged if any enquiries regarding karate are addressed to me as follows: V.C.F. Bell, c/o 12, Maybush Rd, Emerson Park, Hornchurch, Essex. I have several interesting still and action photographs of karate taken in Japan, in Paris, and of our own students taken here, should you be interested in them.

'I look forward to your early reply with much interest, and I am prepared to call on you at your convenience, if you so desire, to discuss the entire matter fully, prior to any publicity you man think fit.

Yours truly, V.C.F. Bell, (National Coach of the Br. Karate Fed.).'

Whilst Nam did, of course, come to England, the planned 'large public displays' involving four non British experts did not, nor did the opening of the IKF or EKU. The planned 'first ever karate display,' also did not take place on the 6th July. This letter is the only reference that the earliest karate training at 12, Maybush Rd, was conducted at week-ends.

line 33 – the missing word is 'He.'

Page 76, line 18 – According to Bell, Brandon worked as a fitter.

line 19 – According to Bell, Dyer worked in an office.

line 19 – Leonard Pearson, 31, toolmaker (18.7.57). Pearson, who lived in Hornchurch, listed swimming, football and cricket as his hobbies, and had practised judo.

line 19 – Brian Miles, 24, policeman (26.6.57). Miles, who lived in Romford at the time, listed philately and marquetry as his hobbies. Attached to his membership form is a newspaper cutting of unknown date (though 1957 or early 1958) and unknown origin, that relates an unfortunate, not to say sad tale. Entitled, 'The Ex – P.C. on a Bicycle,' the piece reads: 'Until recently, a member of the Essex Constabulary, 24-year-old Brian George Miles was fined £15 at Brentwood, Essex. Miles, of Delta Road, Hutton, near Brentwood, pleaded guilty to conduct intended to insult a woman, and asked that seven similar offences should be considered. Mr. Thomas Lavelle, prosecuting, said two women walking in Mount Avenue, Hutton, saw Miles riding a bicycle on which he was behaving improperly. Detective J. H. Powell told the court Miles was appointed a constable in the Essex Constabulary in 1957, and was discharged last month because he did not maintain his studies and was thought not to be an efficient policeman. Two of the offences he admitted were committed while he was in the force. Mr. I.H.A. Millar, defending, said Miles had a good family background. His grandfather and an uncle were policemen.'

Page 78, photograph caption – The *kumite* shown is not from the 1st *Ippon Kata.*

Page 80, line 5 – In fact, as the *BKF Enquiries Register* clearly shows, and astonishing as it may seem, only one individual, a Mr. G. Woodard of Tooting, London, is recorded as enquiring about karate as a consequence of the film. Woodard, who appears as the first entry in the register, did not take up BKF karate.

Page 83, line 38 – According to Bell, Armsby worked as a doorman.

Page 84, line 26 – The date of the marriage should read 1954

A blurred, but important photograph, showing, from left to right: Miles, unknown, Hoang Nam, Bell, Guilfoyle and Pearson – 12, Maybush Rd, Hornchurch (July, 1957) (I/79).

Armsby's BKF licence (1957)

(General Register Office {marriages}: September 1954, Romford, Vol. 5a, p. 1496).

line 26 – The children's names were Rosemary (General Register Office {births}: March 1955, Romford, Vol. 5a, p. 573) and Clive (General Register Office {births}: December 1957, Romford, Vol. 5a, p. 605), respectively. Clive died in 1999, and Rosemary has three children.

Page 85, line 24 – It is recorded in the *BKF Enquiries Register* that a Mr. Dode wrote to the BKF on behalf of Hoang Nam on the 27th June 1963, to note that Nam was 'visiting England and wishes to contact.' The BKF replied with 'all addresses.' Nam, a diabetic, died on the 6th February 1992.

last line – When Nam returned to Paris, he recommended a Scotsman to the BKF. A BKF application for membership form has been discovered for James Anderson, a thirty year old of 'varied' occupation, who had had two tours of duty in the armed forces, and who applied to the BKF on the 26th August 1957. Anderson, who came from Paisley, Renfrewshire, is the first Scotsman to have joined the BKF by two years. Citing Nam in his application form, Anderson, who noted painting, swimming, fishing and climbing as his hobbies, had studied in Paris, but apparently not in karate. Anderson is a real enigma and appears to have vanished nearly as quickly as he appeared. He is, however, almost certainly the first Scotsman to have trained in karate. According to Bell, Anderson worked as a bouncer and had one eye; Bell also noted that he worked as an instructor for the early BKF (though there is no documentary evidence of this) and was very good.

Page 88, line 21 – Bell knew Gunji Koizumi, visiting him, he recalled, at Ebury Place, Victoria, London SW1. Bell informed the author that Koizumi later committed suicide by placing a plastic bag over his head.

Page 98, line 5 – The unknown newspaper is *Reveille*.

Page 104, line 5 – In contrast to the nationally shown film of karate, which, as noted, attracted only one recorded enquiry about the BKF, the article in *Reveille*, a local newspaper, attracted eleven enquiries, one of whom, J. Alibone, joined the BKF in July, 1960.

line 6 – The programme of the first French National Karate Championships, the first karate championships in Europe, shows the following sequence of events:

Premiere Partie

Exemple D'Entrainement Au Karate
Par les Members du Karate Club de France

Demonstrations De Sports
Avec lesquels on confond parfois le karate
Boxe Francaise – M.M. Lafond Pere et Fils
Judo – Les Memberes de l'A.F.J.
Boxe Libre – M.M. Guillemette et Lafond

$^1/_4$ De Finale Du Tournoi National

Assaut du Maitre Mochizuki
Contre deux adversaries en meme temps
Shiwari (Tests de frappe)
Bris de planches et tuiles avec la main, le
dos de la main, le coude, le genou, le pied

Entr'Acte

Buffet dans l'entrée et Livres de Karate et
d'Arts Martiaux

Deuxieme Partie

Katas par MM. Mochizuki et Plee
2e Pin an avec 8 adversaires
4e Pin an
Kushanku

$^1/_2$ Finale Du Tpurnoi National
3 victoires par assaut

Iai-Jutsu par le Maitre Mochizuki

Kendo par le Maitre Mochizuki et
Hamot
Finale Du Tournoi National
1 victoire par assaut

Combats de Bo-Jutsu (baton long)
Nagi-nata (hallebarde)
Canne

Remise des Recompenses

line 31 – In Bell's reply to this (4th November) letter, dated the 11th December 1957, he also enclosed a Christmas card.

line 32 – The date should read 29th January 1958.

line 37 – According to Bell, 'Seydel was a lovely man and I had a lot of respect and time for him.' Bell recalled that Seydel had been a Luftwaffe pilot during the war.

line 37 – Another page to the later letter has been unearthed, and makes interesting reading, if for no other reason than comparative purposes. In page one, Seydel notes that a fire, in the first hour of the New Year, had burned down the family home of two brothers, refugees from Estonia, both of whom were Seydel's students. Fortunately, however, the contents of the cellar, which had been the karate clubroom, had survived, and 'we could save our library and the items installed there.' Seydel continued, 'Our karate at Bad Homburg is progressing slowly. We are still ten, training Monday and Thursday from 19.00 to 21.30 hrs, in a clean and bright *dojo* … with cold and warm water.

'I am not fond of propaganda, although I have settled an agreement with a Boys Scout monthly [magazine] to publish eight continuations (Introduction into Karate-do) with photos and drawings. The first

PROGRAMME

1ᴱᴿ TOURNOI NATIONAL
DE KARATÉ

Combats de boxe libre japonaise à poings et pieds nus
et Festival des Arts Martiaux Français et Japonais
Sabre à 2 mains, Bâton, Canne, Kendo, Boxe Française, Boxe Libre

SALLE DES SPORTS DE
L'ASSOCIATION SPORTIVE
DE LA PRÉFECTURE DE POLICE

16, Rue du Gabon - Paris XIIᵉ
(Métro Porte de Vincennes)

The programme to the 1st French National Karate Championships – 1957
(I/104).

Sparring at the 1st French National Karate Championships – 1957 (I/104)

article will come out in February. A prospectus will be issued to be sent to all German judo clubs (about 230), probably in February or March – just as information to avoid any misunderstanding in the beginning.'

On the second page of the letter, Seydel provides his grading syllabi for 6th and 5th kyu, for he was to give a grading in the first days of February. This information is important, and is given (with some

Trevor Guilfoyle performing a side-kick to Bell – Hornchurch, 1957 (I/98)

words corrected) below:

General condition: 70% of the training hours must have been attended.

6th Kyu:
1. General knowledge about hygiene, training conditions.
2. Ceremonies, behaviour in the *dojo*.
3. Folding up the *keikogi*, knotting the belt.
4. First aid, general knowledge in case of accidents.
5. Karate organisation – all you should know about tasks, rights.
6. Technique of karate.
7. The karate belts and their significance.
8. Composition: 'History of Judo and Karate.'
9. The fundamental positions – description and execution.
10. Movements in *te* and *ashi-waza*.
11. *Uke* [? rest of word unclear].
12. 1st *kata* as *uke* and *tsuki*.
13. Two *yaku-soken* [second word unclear]-*kumite* as *uke* and *tsuki* – five minutes each.

Trevor Guilfoyle counters Bell with a *chudan-empi* – Hornchurch, 1957 (I/98)

5th Kyu:

1. The different kinds of *kumite*.
2. Names (in German) of the practical *te* and *ashi-waza*.
3. Training and meaning of the *kiai*.
4. [Word unclear] – nose-bleeding, hiccup, headache, testicle-injuries.
5. Composition: 'Differences between Judo, Jujitsu and Karate.'
6. Arranged forms of karate movements (*te* and *ashi-waza*).
7. Correct and quick demonstration of the *te-waza*.
8. *Uke* [? rest of word unclear] – good style.
9. Five minutes gymnastics as leader of squad – good description and execution.
10. 2nd *kata* as *uke* and *tsuki*.
11. Fundamental *kumite* and *yaku-soken* [second word unclear] *kumite* as *uke* and *tsuki* – five minutes each.

Seydel also noted in this letter that, 'The article enclosed is the first one published in Germany about karate. The attitude is not yet quite correct (right hand and right foot), but I hope we shall improve our style.' Unfortunately, the said article is lost.

Jurgen Seydel – 1958 (I/104)

Bell did not reply to Seydel's letter of the 29th January, and Seydel sent a postcard on the 31st March 1959, enquiring whether Bell had received it. Bell apologised in his subsequent letter of the 23rd April citing 'pressure of work and family commitments.' This statement was almost certainly true, for Bell liked Seydel, noting that, 'during our short stay in Paris I agree we got on extremely well' (letter of the 23rd

April), and was very interested in how karate in other countries was progressing. Bell was also impressed with the grading syllabi for 6th and 5th kyu. In this letter, Bell also noted that Seydel's offer of placements for English *karateka* in the homes of German *karateka* had not been taken up, but the notion of writing to judo clubs was 'an excellent idea and, if you don't mind, one which we will adopt in Britain.' Bell also wrote that, 'I, too, am not fond of karate propaganda,' and towards the end of the letter noted, 'we, too, are few in number, but very keen, and karate, being a specialised subject, we are not interested in large numbers.' Bell also reaffirmed that, 'our belt holders also practise in the open air on alternative Saturdays in my garden.'

Bell's letter of the 23rd April is particularly important in that it provides us with the syllabi for the first two gradings under the BKF at the time (and before, see *Shotokan Horizon*), which were as follows:

6th Kyu:

1. 10 min. gymnastics and preparatory exercises, the kowtow and *dojo* etiquette.
2. 8 techniques of toughening on the *makiwara*, including the fingers, heel of hand, fist, back of hand, knuckles and elbow.
3. 8 techniques of *kento*, 8 techniques of *shuto*, 8 techniques of *hiji*, 3 techniques of *ashiwaza*.
4. 1st *kata* as *uke* and *tsuki* on both sides, first slowly, then quickly.
5. 3 minute conventional *kumite*.
6. 3 minute *kumite shiai* for one point under contest rules.

To pass, an overall 70 per cent theory and practical.

5th kyu:

Similar to 6th *kyu*, except for five more techniques of *ashiwaza*, the second *kata*, 8 combination techniques of leg and arm, and more contest ability, style and skill in combat, and elementary karate self-defence.

Page 106, line 27 – In a translation of a later undated article in *Budo-Presse,* entitled, 'The Founder of European Karate-Do: Official Interview with Monsieur Henri Plee, 3rd Dan – The Coming of the Japanese Masters,' Plee makes some comments on Murakami: 'Slightly better than Hiroo, his style was crisper and more specialised. His drawback was that he did too many things – judo (4th Dan), kendo and iai ... [and his style] was more nervous, longer, but it was better [than Mochizuki].'

line 28 – Sugiyama and Kondo's first names were Shoji and Mitsuhiro, respectively. Sugiyama was born on the 4th April 1933,

Group shot of students under Master Murakami in Paris – 1958. Back row, left to right: Szpirglas, unknown, unknown, unknown, P. Clarke, Rayner; middle row: Plee, Murakami, Bell, unknown, unknown; front row: Tam Mytho, Swiss representative, Belgian representative (I/118).

in Shizuoka, and began judo in 1946/47. He entered Nihon University in 1954, and travelled to France in 1958, to teach judo.

Page 111, line 29 – According to Bell, Keane, who he recalled was about seventeen when she started karate, worked in an office and baby-sat.

Page 112, line 12 – Higgins and Keane were different people. Bell recalled that Higgins had 'black, curly, floppy hair.'

Page 119, line 25 – According to the *BKF Enquiries Register,* E.J. Harrison recommended four individuals to the BKF in 1959, two in 1960, and one in 1961. We know of at least one recommendation prior to this earlier date, and there are likely to have been more throughout 1958-1961.

Page 122, line 32 – Seydel hadn't been so slow. In a previously lost letter to Bell dated the 10th October 1958, Seydel records that Murakami visited Bad Homburg 'from 26th July until 4th August. Thirty people – from Austria, France, Holland Indo-China and Germany, [including] ten black belt holders (judo), [and] the President of the Austrian Judo Federation, [name unclear, but initial 'F'] ... [and I had] negotiations with the President of the German Judo Union, H. Frantzen, and the Chairman of the German Dan Council, A. Rhode [was in attendance]. Positive results.'

Page 124, line 16 – 'Raynor' is 'Rayner.'

      line 32 – With regard to the Lambourne Hall demonstration, an article on page 3 of the *Romford Recorder/Review*, entitled, 'He Could Have Killed Me,' by Hugh Jones, on Friday, 30th May 1958, Jones (an 'unofficial off-white belt') paired up with Kenshiro Abbe and humorously tells of the exploit. An accompanying photograph shows the hapless and hopelessly outclassed Jones being thrown by the master. In fact, readers of this 'match of the century' had been given previous notice in an unknown newspaper (almost certainly the above), as advertising for the Eastern Counties branch of the BJC.

      In an article entitled, 'Killer Sport Comes to Town,' from an unknown newspaper of unknown date, and by an unknown author, four members of the BKF went on stage at Lambourne Hall to demonstrate karate. Kenshiro Abbe gave a demonstration and over one hundred *judoka* from London and Essex took part in the BJC Championships held that Friday. The results for the championship are given and none of those named appear to have practised karate under the BKF at the time. It is almost certain that the date for this karate display is the 23rd May 1958, though seven (including Bell), not four *karateka* were part of the demonstration, if the event programme was adhered to.

Page 133, line 11 – In a letter of introduction to Vernon Bell, Armstrong wrote that he had 'been in the T.A. Army now for five and a half years and I hold the rank of N.C.O.'

      line 15 – Sen's departure is interesting. Bell wrote to Sen on the 16th July (letter lost) and in his reply (21st July), Sen noted: 'You seem to be obsessed with the idea of being the National Coach and *Shodan* for the British Karate Federation [and that] you have the privilege of saying precisely what [*sic* - should read 'how'] things appear to you, and everybody knows that appearances can be very deceptive. The last time it appeared to you that we were going on our own, although you were entirely wrong, it did not occur to you to apologise to us ...' Sen resigned from the BKF in this short letter. Bell retorted on the 23rd July, raising financial matters, level of technical

Bell leads kicking practice at the Wheatsheaf *dojo* –1958 (I/133)

Bell leads *jodan-age-empi* practice at the Wheatsheaf *dojo* –1958 (I/133)

expertise and Sen's sociability. Bell noted, 'The BKF has no time for wayward members, and as such your resignation is accepted without further consideration.'

It would appear, at least from Sen's perspective, that Bell was concerned about a break-away group from the BKF – if this is so, then it is the first mention of such a split, and its early date is most

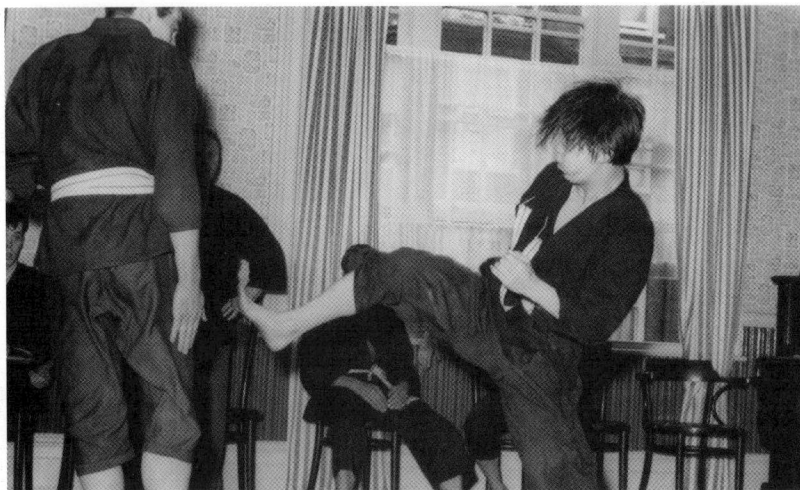

Joe Sen attacks Reg Armstrong with *mae-geri* – Wheatsheaf *dojo*, 1958 (I/133).

surprising. Bell wrote in his letter that he had always been open on all matters with his pupils and that if Sen thought otherwise he was 'a conspirator.'

Sen's departure seems to have had an effect – at least on one fellow student. Rayner, in an undated (though about April, 1959) resignation letter to Bell, wrote: 'I do not feel I am getting enough out of my karate lessons. Ever since Mr. Sen left, who was my partner, as you know, there [has been] nobody to take his place – you see we used to work everything out together; put one another right when the other one went wrong, as it should be. And, I have not done anything new since he has left, which in my estimation is not good for the moral of the members. I would like very much to become a Dan in karate, but under the conditions as they are, I feel that would not be possible.' Rayner planned to go to Australia on the last day of February 1960.

Some five years after leaving the BKF, Monty Russell wrote to Bell (18th February, 1964), noting that, 'I still see Peter Conlan and Joe Sen at times, but they are not doing any karate now' (Russell also wrote that, 'There seem to be plenty of upstarts at the game [karate] now'). In a reply letter dated the 7th May 1964 (the delay being due to it being 'filed away with many others of less importance'), Bell wrote: 'Don't forget you are always welcome to re-join at any time, as is Peter Conlan and also Joe Sen, and all bygones will be bygones. Please remember me to them …'

Scarborough Ippon Judo & Boxing Club

present for the first time in Scarborough

JUDO and BOXING

at the GAIETY THEATRE, ABERDEEN WALK on
THURSDAY, JANUARY 22nd, at 7 p.m.
1959

LEEDS

REG. PARK

DEMONSTRATION OF BODY CULTURE

Worlds Best Developed Man
Mr. UNIVERSE, Mr. WORLD, Mr. EUROPE, etc.

LONDON **Vernon Bell**	Japanese Boxing and Demonstration of Karate as seen on T.V. 1st Dan Karate 3rd Dan Judo	JAPAN **Cliff Gibbs**	3rd Dan Black Belt one of Europe's Leading Experts.
SCARBOROUGH **Peter Jaconelli**	1st Dan Black Belt Judo 2nd Dan Black Belt Ju-Jitsu	SCARBOROUGH **Norman Grundy**	1st Dan Black Belt Judo 2nd Dan Black Belt Ju-Jitsu
SCARBOROUGH BOXING **Tommy Johnson**	A.B.A. Finalist 1957. British Railways Champion England Representative **V.**	DONCASTER **Stuart Pearson**	British Champion. Runner up Empire Games Cardiff, 1958
SCARBOROUGH **Don Robinson**	Ex R.A.F. & Yorkshire Champion. Hull Kingston Rovers Rugby Player **v.**	**Toma Hansom**	Tripolitania and North Africa Champion

AND SUPPORTING CONTESTS.

P TICKETS - 10/- (ringside) 6/- 4/- 2/-
Tickets on sale from all Club Members, Gaiety Theatre, and Jaconelli Shops

Scarborough Ippon Judo and Boxing Club poster featuring BKF karate –
1959 (I/145).

Page 140, line 24 – Guilfoyle did not die on active service with the SAS.

      line 36 – The faded, light orange programme reveals that, 'Karate and Karate-Do' was the first feature on after Neville Powley, ITV/BBC compere and producer, had been introduced by Wally Wright. Following the karate demonstration, Rueb Martin and Ernest Bevan gave a display of duo dancing. There were fifteen items on the programme that evening.

Page 144, line 36 – At the time *The Manual of Karate* was published, Harrison was living at 19, Mornington Avenue, West Kensington, London, W14.

Page 150, line 2 – A note from Plee to Bell has been discovered that post-dates the disagreement. Undated, handwritten, but from or after 1962, Plee wrote on the back of his white professional card, so: 'I have been happy to see that we have both forgotten some misunderstandings. I hope that you have found in karate many good things as I have found, especially under Mr. Ohshima, teaching a kind of genius.' Plee's card reveals him to be: '4th Dan judo, 3rd Dan karate, 2nd Dan aikido, 1st Dan kendo.'

Page 156, line 33 – In a letter from Murakami to Bell, dated the 20th September 1959, we learn that he was under the impression that Bell was interested in publishing an aikido book he'd either written, which the tone of the letter suggests, or intended to write. The letter deals with terms. To the author's knowledge, Murakami never had a book published on any subject.

line 37 – Another, later case, was Seydel's book, *Karate*, which at the time (1962) was priced at 22.80 Deutschmarks. Seydel wrote to Bell on the 30th July 1963, in reply to a now lost letter from Bell. Seydel wrote: 'Your idea of translating and publishing my manual in England would be great, and I think we might get a good agreement.' In reply to another lost letter from Bell, Seydel wrote on the 6th September 1963 that, 'with a book of this sort you never will be able to collect a fortune. It took me two years to write the text and make the drawings. The main purpose was, however, to help spread karate in our country.' A number of later letters between Bell and Seydel refer to the project.

Page 157, line 9 – Quotes from Terry Wingrove's two references will be given as testament to his character at the time of joining the BKF. Both come from employees of Cossor Radar and Electronics Limited and both are dated the 30th June 1959. The first comes from L. Mawson: 'We understand the above named [Wingrove] has applied to you for a course of training in karate. He is serving an apprenticeship with this company and has been with us for two years during which time he has proved to be well behaved and of good character. We see no reason why he should not be accepted for a training course.'

The second reference comes from a P. Kirby: 'I have known the above named for two years of his employment at Cossor Radar and Electronics Ltd., Harlow. During this period of Drawing Office training, Mr. Wingrove has come under my direct supervision and I have found him to be honest, reliable, and a conscientious worker. He is keen and quick to learn and able to accept responsibility. I have, therefore, no hesitation in recommending Mr. Wingrove for membership of the British Karate Federation.'

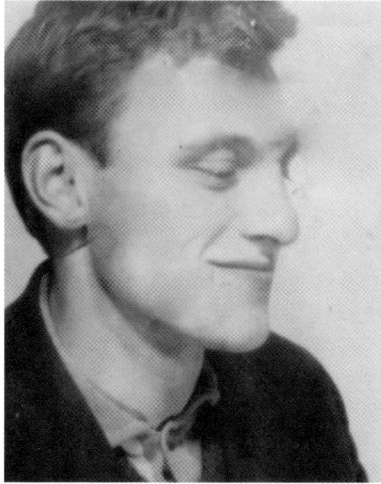

The photograph that Terry Wingrove submitted with his BKF application form (I/157).

line 15 – According to Bell, Shepherd, who was an office worker, was one of the best BKF students.

Page 159, line 18 – Bell noted the *dojo* was under the AJA, but when the author attended, it was affiliated to the BJC.

Page 160, line 1 – Vernon Bell recalled: 'I also taught judo and ju-jitsu to the SAS at their Euston Square barracks. I suppose that would be at the end of the 1950s. I found them to be a strange collection of individuals to be honest. Wingrove accompanied me. We trained on mats about eighteen inches thick. Once an attack had been blocked or avoided, I taught the blow-throw-blow sequence – a strike to the head or chest to cause disorientation, then a throw to the floor, with the opponent often landing on his head, and finishing the attacker off once on the floor. With the opponent prostrate, I taught the Principle of Three – a *shuto* to the neck, followed by a punch to the chest, and finally a strike to the lower abdomen/groin region.

I remember on one occasion I was teaching the SAS and a soldier walked in with a grenade in his hand, pulled the pin, and said, 'Anyone dare me to drop it?' Nobody said a word and he walked out. Was it some kind of joke? I don't think so. The atmosphere was such that I reckon he would have released the clip if anyone had dared him. Crazy … and chilling.'

line 24 – After Murakami split from Plee, he appears to have aligned himself with Jim Alcheik. A letter from Seydel to Bell dated the 6th June 1959, makes this clear, and notes that Murakami's address at the time as being: c/o M. Mai Ngoo Lan, 62 rue du Chateau, Asmieres, Seine.

Page 164, top photograph caption – the student standing to Murakami's left is not Armstrong.

Page 169, line 4 – Peter McEvoy, 28, engine room attendant (1.6.69) – from Dinnington, near Sheffield.
       line 5 – According to Bell, Milner was a plumber by trade.
       line 6 – Gerald Dougherty, 33, decorator (-.8.59). Dougherty lived in Oxford and was an Upminster club member.
       line 7 – John Farkas, 38, salesman (18.10.59). Farkas, lived in Rugby, and was an Upminster club member. According to Bell, he was a Hungarian refugee, and acted as a witness to Bell's second marriage. Bell also recalled that he believed that Farkas started a karate club up in his home town in Warwickshire.

Page 170, line 24 – Robert Wardle. Vernon Bell did not take kindly to people who trained on an irregular basis, nor did he mince his words. In an undated letter, Wardle, in reply to letters by Bell, wrote: 'I have been unable to attend karate classes on the past two Sundays as I have injured my foot and was unable to walk. I was going to attend classes this Sunday, but in view of the two letters which I have received from you which I didn't like at all, I have decided that if this is the way you speak to your pupils I do not wish to attend anymore. I am very sorry that I have to make this decision because I am still very keen on karate. But owing to your attitude I am afraid I cannot.'
       line 25 – J. Banfield, 26, dock worker (17.5.59), who, according to Bell, was a carpenter with a withered right leg, and had come to karate from ju-jitsu. Frederick Buckman, 40, representative (16.7.59); Patrick Hill, 18, shop assistant (3.9.59); Dennis Smith, 43, gardener (-.-.59).
       line 26 – Donald Sheehan should read 'Ronald Sheehan.'
       line 30 – According to Bell, Ghose, who was Indian, worked as a clerk.
       line 31 – Selwyn Herzenberg, 24, engineer (23.6.60).
       line 40 – Barry Langton, 30, musician (5.10.60). Langton was a judo 1st kyu.

last line – Anthony Buckley, 20, trainee surveyor (12.12.1960).

Page 171, line 7 – According to Bell, Williams was shot dead in his car in the 1960s, in what appears to have been a gangland killing.

Page 175, line 1 – In a letter to Bell dated the 23rd January 1957, a certain W. Reeve, gives the address of the Abbe Judo School as: St. James Parish Hall, Collier Street, London, N.1. This is almost certainly where the BKF trained.

Page 177, line 10 – Gille appears to have wasted no time in his attempt to establish karate in Liverpool. On the 24th September 1959, he issued a circular to work colleagues. The entire circular, which is not strictly accurate, will be reproduced here owing to its historical importance. The text has been grammatically corrected in places and all underlined upper-case words have been retained. It reads:

'Ladies and Gentlemen,

I held a meeting on Wednesday 23rd inst. in the Works canteen, the object being to determine the number of employees interested in joining a Karate-Do section. This was done at your recommendation, and I now submit for your consideration the names and addresses of those interested.

Unfortunately, a recent B.B.C. television programme dealing with Japan, included a short item on karate as practised as a martial art in Japan, and if you saw this programme you may have gained the wrong impression of the SPORT, and I therefore ask you to give me an audience, or at least hear with the following attempt to explain the SPORT.

JU-JUTSU is a killing technique as practised in old Japan and means GENTLE ART – the word JU being GENTLE and JUTSU being ART. JUDO is a sport based upon the killing art of JU-JUTSU. Again JU being GENTLE and Do being WAY – the GENTLE WAY.

Between the two world wars, many people thought of judo as a killing technique, believing that it was, in fact, ju-jutsu. Indeed, the methods of dislocating, strangling and killing are taught in judo, but you will all realise that they are not practised, and judo is fast becoming a national sport. Fencing teaches the technique of killing, but one does not practise with a real rapier on an unprotected man.

So KARATE is a killing technique, the word KARATE means 'EMPTY HAND', but KARATE-DO is the sport based on the technique of <u>KARATE</u>. Again, <u>DO</u> being the <u>WAY</u>.

The British Karate Federation is a responsible, registered national body concerned with the promotion of <u>KARATE-DO</u> as a sport. It controls the sport rigidly and sensibly, and in answer to my recent enquiry (made for your committee's benefit), the Technical Director and National Coach states that in London they have not bothered with insurance, as they have not considered it necessary, and [he] assures me that, in his considered opinion, there is less chance of injury from the practice of karate-do than in any other martial art (judo, etc). I have the letter here for the committee's inspection.

It is my hope that the committee will remember me as a sensible and responsible person, and you may rest assured that I would not dream of embarking upon a scheme that would bring any discredit upon our club.

I have some thirty people who are interested in the formation of the section, which can be a financially sound and unique branch of our sports and social club. Should you discover it to be otherwise, I will undertake to disband it and repay any expense the sports and social club may have incurred.

Hoping that I have shed some light upon the subject and that you will give the matter your impartial consideration, I am, Ladies and Gentlemen,

Yours Sincerely.'

line 21 – '8th' should read '18th.'

Page 178, line 2 – In a letter dated the 14th May 1962, Bell wrote to Gille that: 'With effect from today you are personally re-graded to full 4th kyu in recognition of your services and devotion to the BKF, as well as for your enthusiasm in technical matters, and in view of the leadership displayed in assisting me ...' Gille resigned from the BKF in 1962. His letter of resignation is undated, but he wrote to Bell: 'As you have not replied to my last letter and you have made my position here rather intolerable, I regret that I must ask you to accept this letter as my resignation. I have handed all BKF documents over to G. Galletley...' One cannot help but conclude, given the correspondence, that this was a singularly unfortunate affair.

Bell remembered Gille so: 'His heart was in the right place and I'm sad our relationship ended as it did, because looking back it wasn't necessary. He was an intelligent man, genuinely interested in Shotokan. He believed in it and did his best to establish the art in Liverpool.' The story of the early BKF Liverpool *dojo* is told in the author's, *The Liverpool Red Triangle (1959-1966) and the Formation of the Karate Union of Great Britain.*

Page 181, line 16 – A John McGuffie, of unknown age and occupation, applied to join the BKF in an unknown day in September 1964. His form was found in a mixed batch, and one assumes he was a member of the Liverpool *dojo*.

    line 17 – More should read 'Moore' (and on page 309).

Page 182, photograph caption – the three unknowns, kneeling, are, left to right: Roy Stephens (Liverpool), Bartholomew Lynch (Dublin) and Trevor McCamley (Dublin). The unknown, standing, extreme left, is John Robinson (Dublin).

    line 7 – Smith's age was 20.

    last line – Other Liverpool BKF members that have been uncovered (with dates, if known) are: N. Barooah (1962), A. Burgess (1965), T. Burgess (there is a Burgess of the Rotherham *dojo*), H. Cope, R. Morris (1965), E. Murphy (1963), R. Murray (1965), P. Pyros, C. Rees, H. Rush, J. Shaw (1965 {there is a J. Shaw of the Saltcoats *dojo* and there is a Shaw of the Rotherham *dojo*}), R. Sword, N. Thanes (writing unclear – this is almost certainly N. Thomas from the Blackpool *dojo*) and J. Williams (there is a J. Williams of the York *dojo*). Amongst the non-active members are J. Killilea and D. McQuire.

Page 183, line 17 – According to Bell, Harris was a company director.

    line 17 – At this time a new BKF *dojo* opened up in Stoke-on-Trent, run by Edward John Shaw, a twenty-six year old research chemist, who applied for BKF membership on the 10th June 1960. Shaw joined the BKF a judo *Shodan* from Abbe, and had been a semi-finalist in the BJA Midland Area Championships in 1958. He trained and instructed at the Kasami Shin Judo Kwan, Half-Way House, Anchor Road, Longton, Stoke-on-Trent. Bell recalled that Shaw was: 'A very capable man, most affable and conscientious.' Four members of the judo club joined the BKF (grades given in brackets): Graham James (4th kyu), 24, china caster (17.1.61); Peter Ruddle (3rd kyu), 17, joiner (17.1.61); Malcolm Smith (3rd kyu), 17, engineer (11.1.61); Alistair Tranter (1st kyu), 18, schoolboy (12.6.60). In fact, there were two BKF Stoke *dojos*, the second appeared six years later and is covered in Vol. II.

Edward Shaw – BKF Stoke *dojo,* 1960

Page 188, line 39 – Patrick Butler, 32, salesman (16.7.60). Butler had reached 2nd kyu in judo at the time of his application.

      line 40 – Thomas Laverick, 33, painter (15.7.60). Like Butler, Laverick, though ungraded, was studying judo at the Tamashimu Judo Kwan in South Shields.

      last line – Royston Edward Salmon, 31, electrician (30.6.60). R.E. Salmon had a brother, Royston Graham Salmon (24, paint sprayer {19.5.59}), who also trained with the BKF. Both Salmons were private students of Bell.

Page 189, line 4 – 'E. Stoke' is likely to be Edward Stokoe, a forty-five year old dance band leader from Newcastle-upon-Tyne, who applied to join the BKF on the 1st July 1960.

Page 191, line 11 – According to Minoru Kawawada, the *dojo* opened on the 20th March, 1955 (Wight, K. *Minoru Kawawada, 7th Dan JKA.* {*Shotokan Karate Magazine*, No. 54, p. 18-19}).

Page 192, line 30 – Richardson worked in an office.

      line 31 – According to Bell, Wijesundera was the son of the High Commissioner of Ceylon (Sri Lanka), in London.

Page 193, photograph caption – the student behind Wingrove is Stephen Morgan.

      last line – Michael Dinsdale, 25, labourer (6.12.60) from Ipswich.

Master Murakami delivering an *ushiro-geri* on Bob Buckner at the 1960 Summer School in Scarborough (I/188).

last line – Kenneth Mansfield, 28, driver (11.12.60). Mansfield was a judo 2nd kyu.

Page 202, photograph caption – the date is 25th May, 1963, at the BKF Dublin *dojo* (CIE Engineering Works, Inchicore).

Page 203, line 11 – Bell used to provide an additional article for inclusion in the printed programme for his 'multi-art' demonstrations. An undated copy of this has been found which, Bell assured the author, is from the late Fifties or very early Sixties. The article began: 'Today the audience will see several of the different Japanese martial arts of which there are many different forms, but we will display those of judo, ju-jitsu, aikido and karate-do, which are the most commonly practised in Japan today. I will give a brief summary of each of these four arts to enlighten the onlooker.' As *Shotokan Dawn* concerns itself solely with karate, the fourth section will only be reproduced here with slight grammatical corrections. It is not well written and contains inaccurate information. Bell wrote:
'You who are the founder of karate in Britain, and who has trained

Roy Salmon blocking James Trotter's *oi-zuki* attack – Ilford Baths, 1960

the first pupils in this country, tell me <u>exactly</u>, 'What is Karate-Do?' ... Until recently, I used to launch into a long explanation – karate is not an art of defence like others, for it was created to kill, to wound (hurt) seriously or to disable. It is not strictly speaking Japanese. It was born in Okinawa, an island south of Japan as far away from the 'capital' as Sicily is from Britain. Invaded by the Japanese seven hundred years ago, its inhabitants saw (found) themselves forbidden, absolutely, to possess arms. In order to struggle against the invading forces, they transformed Chinese boxing – three thousand years old – into a martial art; a war sport if you prefer. Today, it is considered in Japan that a karateist, without any arms other than his hands and feet, is more dangerous than a man armed with a knife The police and Japanese Army, as well as the United States Army, have officially adopted it since 1945. I used to think that my questioner was enlightened, but it was only then that the questions began. 'It is judo. No. How does it compare with judo? What difference between it and French boxing? Chinese boxing? Now, I make this answer, which is for you – karate was an <u>Art of War</u>. Karate-Do is a <u>Sport of War</u> destined to save our life and perfect our personality, but all those who practise it continue to call [it] their sport karate. Karate is free boxing in which everything is allowed. Not only striking with the fist, four fingers, elbows, knees, ball of the foot, the heel, the head, etc., but also to upset and finish the adversary by striking him to the ground. You notice EVERYTHING IS PERMITTED. There is one single convention – NOT TO STRIKE REALLY or do harm, but to show that victory is indisputable. It is therefore free boxing and fencing with the bare hand. Bare feet, too.'

Page 206, line 14 – Entry 92 of *The BKF Register of Enquiries* shows that Thompson's letter was dated the 3rd January 1961, and that a reply was sent on the 17th January 1961. Literature sent to Thompson was: a letter, leaflet, circular, application form, and application certificate.

John Clark also sent a letter to the BKF (entry 101), applying for membership on the 25th January, and a reply was sent on the 8th February.

line 34 – A Pat McHugh, 19, formerly of the Services, but at the time of his application to the BKF (1.11.65) believed to be a barman, though on a second completed application (26.11.65) his occupation is unclear, provides us with the only surviving application refused by Bell (though there is anecdotal information to suggest that

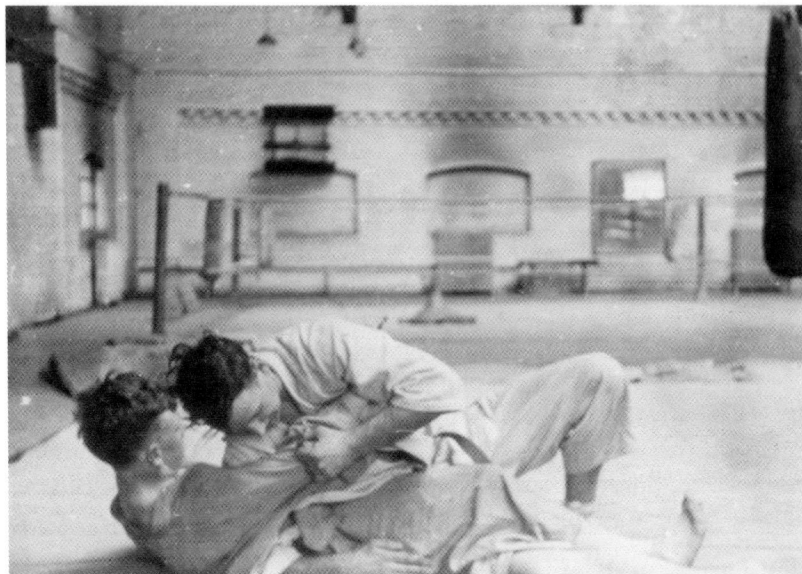

Gordon Thompson, on top, practising judo at the York Railway Institute Gymnasium in 1954/55. It was at this *dojo* that karate was first practised in York. Thompson and fellow *judoka*, John Clark, formed the BKF York Branch in 1961. It was at YRIG that Thompson first met Steve Cattle, Tony Aydon and Patrick O'Donovan (I/204).

he dissuaded people from applying before issuing them with a BKF application form). In December, 1965, Bell wrote: 'With reference to your recent application for licence of this Federation, I am directed to inform you that from the particulars submitted on your application form, that your application for membership has not been approved by this Federation, and accordingly I am unable to offer you a course of training. Naturally this non-acceptance of membership is without prejudice and nothing is to prevent you from re-applying in the New Year in the same manner.'

Page 207, line 27 – Whilst Ainsworth is credited with introducing BKF karate to Scotland, he certainly wasn't the first Scotsman to train in the art. William McSkimming, a twenty-five year old fireman from Troon, with interests in judo, boxing and weightlifting, applied for BKF membership on the 17th August 1959, thus pre-dating Ainsworth by nearly two years. James Anderson (see earlier), of course, pre-dates McSkimming by a further two years.

Master Murakami (far left) instructing at the St. Osyth Summer School, 1961. David Williams (left) and Barry Sheppard are in the foreground. Alan Ruddock can just be made out centre, behind the student with glasses (I/213).

Page 211, photograph caption – Alan Ruddock, from Dublin, fourth from left.

Page 214, line 33 – Graham McLeod, 20, tyre fitter (4.4.61), from Exeter. McLeod wrote to Bell on the 22nd January 1962 (letter now lost) noting the possibility of opening a BKF Branch in the West Country. Bell replied on the 25th January providing details as to how this could be achieved. However, the *dojo* never materialised, and in a forthright letter of the 6th April 1963, Bell wrote to McLeod dismissing him from the BKF due to non-payment of his licence renewal fee.

Whilst McLeod was the first BKF student from the West Country, he certainly wasn't the first to make an enquiry, for that distinction goes to Charles Case, a Plymouth dock worker, who wrote to Bell on the 21st August 1959 asking for details, noting that he thought that karate could become popular in that part of the country. Case, who ran the Otani Judo Academy and had nine clubs under his jurisdiction, was a 2nd Dan in judo from Abbe, and intended taking his 3rd Dan the following month. Case, who sent one pound and sixpence on the 27th September 1959 as a membership fee for the remaining part of the year, noted that he had successfully graded to 3rd Dan, and reiterated that he felt that karate would be successful in Devon and Cornwall. A doctor's certificate and two references, followed, but Case wrote in a later, undated letter, that he had not heard from Bell. Bell did write (letter lost), and the last correspondence between the two men to have survived comes from Case dated the 2nd January 1960. It is clear that the three main problems were distance, Case's heavy schedule (Bell offered Case a date to come to Upminster, but Case was unable to do so because of his judo commitments, as his letter of the 11th November 1959 reveals), and lack of financial resources on Case's part to enable him to get Bell down to Plymouth for a course. As far as the author is aware, Case never became a member of the BKF, and it does seem that, potentially, a great opportunity was missed for both parties, and, of course, for Shotokan in Great Britain.

    line 36 – Two trainees on the course were Eric Sullivan, 29, company director (8.8.61), and Reginald Torr, 31, managing director (11.8.61). Sullivan and Torr not only lived in St.Osyth, but resided in the same street, Point Clear Road.

Page 215, line 37 – Thompson recalled, once the York *dojo* was up and running: 'The first time we had … [Terry Wingrove] … in our ignorance we had arranged to train for two, four-hour sessions – that's right, two, four-hour sessions. Poor mad fools we were. Anyway, Terry made no comment, but did it. We seemed to be doing a lot of exercises, but what the hell, we were young and fit and we could take it. Bunny hops formed a large part of these [exercises]. After seeing Terry off on the train, we went to our usual pub and leant on the door till it opened. We were already stiffening up, and after about an hour we could hardly get off the stools or chairs – our knees were that stiff. It got so bad that just negotiating a single low step … was an obstacle to be dreaded. It took three days for this stiffness to wear off and is still remembered today when some of us old members bump into each other.'

Page 217, line 3 – 'Patsby' should read 'Patsky.'

Page 218, line 7 – Ashton's initial is 'R'.

Page 219, line 12 – The first correspondence with Lt. Kenny is a letter written by Bell on the 26th October 1961, noting that, subsequent to a telephone conversation, he (Bell) would 'be pleased to accept this appointment [karate instructor] on an indefinite basis

Art Malia – BKF Denham *dojo*, 1961 (I/220)

commencing instruction on Saturday, 4th November 1961, on the following arrangement: (a) class of unlimited numbers for three hours each week from 11 a.m. to 2.00 p.m. (b) the agreed fees to be on a salaried basis of twenty-five shillings per hour, payable weekly by cheque, payable to myself, and to include petrol allowance at five shillings per gallon, being, fifty miles each way at twenty-five miles per gallon, i.e., £1.'

line 14 – The date of the 31st March was the initial date for closure of classes at Denham, but this was later extended to the 30th June.

line 19 – 'Echeverna' should read 'Echeverria' (and on pages 220, 225, 306).

line 20 – Smith's initial is 'D.'

Page 220, line 7 – 'Winichx' may read 'Wirichx' or 'Werichx' (and on pages 225, 311).

Page 223, photo caption – 'Eric' should be spelt 'Erik' and 'Monski' should read 'Manski.'

line 17 – The letter to Robinson was dated the 20th March 1962.

Page 224, line 36 – The date and times of this course are confirmed in Bell's letter to Lt. Kenny dated the 1st June 1962. This is an interesting letter for it reveals that Bell taught karate at the USAF Base at South Ruislip, noting that he had 'recommenced on Saturday, 21st April 1962, at 1.00 pm,' but noting that he had received no remuneration for his services.

Page 225, line 1 – 'Ulrich' should read 'Ulich' (and on pages 229 and 311).

Page 228, photograph caption – the date is 25th May, 1963, at the BKF Dublin *dojo* (CIE Engineering Works, Inchicore).
　　　　line 4 – Confirmation of the extension to closure of the Denham BKF club comes from another letter by Baker to Bell dated the 13th August 1962, when Bell was paid forty-nine pounds and ten shillings covering Saturday instruction for ten weeks commencing the 28th April and concluding the 30th June. Baker, quoting from his earlier letter, once again reiterated his appreciation of Bell's services.

Page 229, line 21 – 'Baumgartner' may be 'Baumgarther.'
　　　　line 24 – 'Wood' should read 'Ward' (and on page 311).

Page 230, line 24 – Another newspaper clipping has been found with regards to Robinson. Entitled, 'Spang Sgt Picked Karate Club Coach,' undated and short, it notifies readers that Robinson 'has become the first member of the U.S. Air Force to be elected as a coach of the German Karate Federation.'

Page 232, line 11 – The last of the correspondence to have survived is a letter from Robinson to Bell dated the 5th April 1962, in which Robinson expresses sorrow at the closing of BKF karate at Denham, noting, 'you may be assured that I am aware of what is going on in the karate movement in the U.S. Forces.' Robinson proposed that should the BKF ask the American Embassy in London, there was a better chance that he and members of his club could visit, and that an exhibition might be arranged for U.S. Air Force officials.
　　　　last line – Another well known pop singer turned actor to at least sample karate in the early Sixties [probably 1962] was a young man in his early twenties, Terence Nelhams, better known to millions as Adam Faith. Walter Seaton recalled: 'Faith once visited our [Middlesbrough] *dojo* and did a small amount of training and had some publicity photo's taken for the local paper, the *Evening Gazette*.

Fred Kidd – BKF Middlesbrough
dojo, 1960 (I/236).

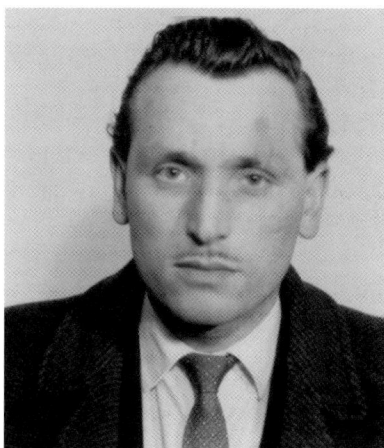

Walter Seaton – BKF Middlesbrough
dojo, 1962 (I/236).

One of them was published and the reporter at the time was six feet seven inch Eric Sumner, who was a senior student at the club … [Faith] did tell us that he had been training somewhere in Scarborough and I think it must have been a Shotokan *dojo*.' This *dojo* is unknown, was not part of the BKF, and the reference does not refer to a BKF Summer School. Vernon Bell did not know that Faith, who died in 2003, had visited the Middlesbrough *dojo*.

Page 235, photograph caption – the photograph was taken in the CIE Hall, Inchicore, Dublin (25th May, 1963). BKF members are, left to right: Trevor McCamley, Bell, Bartholomew Lynch, Edward Swendell, Murakami, John Robinson, Michael O'Doherty, Alan Ruddock.

Page 236, line 10 – Kidd applied for membership to the BKF on the 13th June 1960, aged forty-one, and a labourer by occupation. He had served in the army for ten years, reaching the rank of bombardier. At the time of his application, he listed judo and boxing as his hobbies, and was the founder of the Middlesbrough Judo Club (in 1955) and the Buller Judo Club in New Zealand.

    line 12 – At the time of his application, Seaton was aged twenty-five, had reached the rank of corporal whilst in the army, and listed his occupation as 'branch manager.'

Page 238, photograph – The photograph was taken at the CIE Hall, Inchicore, Dublin (25th May, 1963).

Page 243, line 28 – A report in an unknown newspaper, of unknown date, by an uncredited writer, provides us with an account of Suzuki's weekend's karate training at a gymnasium in Boundary Road, Middlesbrough. Suzuki's age is given as thirty-seven, and, if this is so, then the date of the piece is, because of Suzuki's birthday (27th April), most likely to be 1965, but could be early 1966.

Page 244, line 36 – 'Baver' should read 'Bauer' (and on page 305).

Page 245, photograph caption – the photograph was taken in the CIE Hall, Inchicore, Dublin (25th May, 1963). BKF members are, left to right: Anthony Clarke, Michael O'Doherty, Bartholomew Lynch, Trevor McCamley, Bell (in background), John Robinson and Alan Ruddock (obscured by Murakami).

    line 2 – 'Furlonge' may read 'Furlonger.'

    line 9 – James Kay, 18, apprentice bricklayer (15.1.64); Stanley Kidd, 15, schoolboy (5.2.62); David Lewis, 20, labourer (1.2.62); Rosemary Maine, 17, languages student (25.6.64); Frederick Maughan, 35, stevedore (8.7.64); Edward Melling, 20, apprentice electrician (24.9.63); Ronald Mitchell, 17, French polisher (19.4.62); Dermot Muldoon, 22, driver (2.5.62); Trevor Overfield, 20, plumber (8.4.64); Brund Pacitto, 19, motor fitter (16.5.63); Frederick Parkinson, age and occupation unknown (5.8.63); Alan Paterson, 20, apprentice electrician (14.5.64); William Pears, 31, policeman (18.2.64); Edwin Pettler, 23, laboratory tester (-.-.63); Kenneth Sharp, 27, plater (10.1.63); John Sharpe, 16, coach builder (8.1.63); James Smith, 38, rigger (2.3.64); Denis Southall, 39, stevedore (10.7.62); John Sparkes, 19, laboratory steward (5.7.62); Norman Sudron, 34, P.E. teacher (21.5.64); Eric Sumner, 19, reporter (1.4.62); Carol Tombs, 14, schoolgirl (21.5.64); Peter Towse, 17, apprentice electrician (7.4.64); Gordon Turnbull, 21, commercial trainee (29.1.61); Alan Wheatley, 19, apprentice fitter (17.2.64); George Williamson, 30, TV engineer (10.5.62); Doreen Would, 21, upholsteress (18.2.64).

Page 248, line 3 – 'Holan' should read 'Horkan' (and on page 307). 'Summer' should read 'Sumner' (and on pages 257 and 310).

    line 4 – Of Sumner, Seaton reflected: 'Whenever anyone had a free-fight with Eric (and I did, many times) the main problem was [because of his great height] defending against his downward elbow strikes to the top of the head.'

line 9 – 'Dacosla' is likely to be 'Da Costa' (and on page 306).

line 35 – Correspondence exists between Bell and Charles Naylor concerning this course. The Liverpool club were having trouble raising sufficient funds to cover the intended Murakami training (letter from Naylor dated the 1st October 1962). The course was from 10.00 a.m. to 6.00 p.m., excluding lunch. Murakami was to be paid at £2. 10. 0. per hour, and with petrol at five shillings a gallon, the sum to be found by the Liverpool members was £24 (letter from Bell dated 4th October 1962). Murakami and Bell were pleased to accept Naylor's hospitality at Arnian Road, Rainford, Lanchashire.

Page 251, line 6 – According to Bell, Stoker worked as a driver.

Page 256, line 8 – 'Bryans' should read 'Bryant' (and on page 306).

line 12 – According to Bell, Bounds was a tradesman.

line 13 – 'Glinnen' should read 'Glinnan' (and on page 305). Lawrence Glinnan, 25, taxi cab proprietor (30.10.62).

– Ronald Mills, 21, apprentice engineer (24.11.62).

line 16 – According to Bell, Pressman worked as a taxi driver.

line 18 – According to Bell, De Silva was Ceylonese.

Page 257, line 25 – On the 26th June 1963, Bell received a letter from a certain Harry Schaefer, who wrote: 'I am a member of the German Karate Federation and have obtained your address from Mr. Jurgen Seydel. I have now been in England for a few days and am staying with my sister … [in Faversham, Kent]. I shall be returning to Germany on the 12th or 13th July, and before that date I hope to have the pleasure of seeing your karate school in London. Would you please be so kind and let me know when your school is open in order that I may take the opportunity of visiting your school.' A note on the top of this letter reveals that Bell replied on the 27th June, and the words, 'visit Horseshoe, Tues, 2/7/63 8.30 p.m.' also appear. However, Bell informed the author that Schaefer never did attend a BKF class.

line 27 – 'Pelter' may be 'Pettler.'

N. Pressman performing *gedan-bari* at the Upminster *dojo* – 1963

Laurie Barnett and Alan Chuntz performing *age-uke* at the Upminster *dojo* – late 1962/early 1963.

Page 262, line 3 – Geoffrey Bryant, 18, apprentice plumber (2.11.62). Bryant was a member of the London *dojo*, but broke his leg in an accident in June 1964. This incident appears to have put paid to further karate training. In his last letter to Bell, dated 14th July 1964, Bryant makes reference to a Victoria *dojo* that Bell was presumably trying to set-up.

line 8 – A newspaper article entitled, 'Karate Popular in York Club,' by Malcolm Huntington, in an unknown newspaper of unknown date, can be located here. The article is accompanied by a photograph of John Clark performing the opening move from *Heian Nidan* to an *oi-zuki* attack by Gordon Thompson. Both are recorded as 4th kyu. Thompson had just received his 4th kyu from Murakami and Clark received his 5th kyu on the same occasion (see above). Clark received his 4th kyu under Kanazawa on the 9th July 1965. It is therefore unlikely that they were ever 4th kyus together. The photograph certainly predates Kanazawa's arrival, so the photo is likely to be late 1963 or early 1964, as 'January' is mentioned with regard to a coming beginners' course.

Gordon Thompson practising *gedan-barai* in *zenkutsu-dachi* at the INL Working Men's Club – 1962/63 (I/258).

Page 267, line 38 – In a letter to Seydel dated the 28th November 1963, we get further confirmation that Bell intended to meet Mochizuki. Bell had hoped to see Seydel in Paris, but this was not to be, and in a letter dated the 3rd December 1963, we learn that Seydel was forced to work at a difficult time for his firm, the Bad Homburg Casino, which we learn in a later letter (Seydel to Bell dated the 19th February 1965) concerned the renewal of their gaming licence. In a

Gordon Thompson facing the *makiwara* – York, 1963 (I/258)

letter to Bell dated the 15th December 1963, from Uwe Fullgrabe, we learn that Seydel 'has to change his job and has resigned the Technische Kommission of the DKB. Therefore, in Germany, we are in a very difficult situation because now there is no competent Shotokan instructor.' In fact, this information was not correct, and Seydel kept his position. Bell replied to Seydel in a letter of the 10th February 1964, and in response to worries by Seydel regarding, 'a lot of trouble with US Army black-belts from every system and school, ranking from 1st to 5th Dan, opening classes with Germans and splitting up karate in every possible direction,' Bell noted: 'We fully sympathise with you in your difficulties, but as yet we have had very little interference from these great American boys with their high grades and fancy systems.'

Page 273, line 9 – A letter from George Galletly, BKF Liverpool Branch Officer, to Bell, dated the 22nd December 1963, notes: 'I understand that you had a good weekend in Paris, but it seems a bit unfair to have pitted 3rd kyus against 1st kyus, especially as we do not do free-practise [freestyle]! Anyway, all's well that end's well.'

      line 29 – Selected, historically pertinent and interesting points from the minutes of the European Congress for Karate, which is believed to have met at 12, Rue Lecuirot, Paris (14e), are:

'Mr. Stas expressed surprise that karate had become affiliated to judo federations. He thought that it should be autonomous.'

'Mr. Delcourt … insisted that only contributed judo federations could bring the necessary help to the growth of karate … Mr. Delcourt was utterly convinced that karate would never develop in Europe if there was a certain degree of animosity between the two [judo/karate] sports.'

'Mr. Cherix agreed with this [Delcourt's] opinion and stated that, in Switzerland, karate has also become affiliated to the Swiss Federation for Judo and that, after a difficult beginning due to misunderstanding, difficulties have vanished and Swiss karate has made a promising start. In Belgium and England the official federations for judo have begun to take an interest in karate.'

'Mr. Sebban declared that isolationism could not produce any result. It is necessary to be affiliated to a federation while keeping a managerial autonomy.'

'Mr. Delcourt pointed out the difficulties French karate had met with foreign experts and for this reason would not like the European Union for Karate to follow the same path.'

'Mr. Stas declared that an agreement would be reached with difficulty if people or experts, who had formerly developed karate in Europe were put aside on principle. He found an agreement on this point impossible, but would agree if these experts were to be told of the Union with an eventual view to affiliate themselves to it.'

'Mr. Sebban … the Belgian representatives do not understand the interference of a judo federation in the affairs of karate.'

'Mr. Delcourt mentioned the existence of the ex-European Federation for Karate and regretted that French karate had not been asked to become a member.'

'Mr. Stas mentioned Mr. Schiffelers who, according to him, in Belgium is uniquely representative of his own club. From all this came out the fact that the great amount of small associations in Belgium would be the cause of some difficulty in establishing firm agreements ...'

'Mr. Kiltz (Germany) declared that the German Judo Federation seemed very hostile to karate.'

'Mr. Delcourt mentioned his attitude towards the representatives of the smaller dissenting groups and mentioned that the hardening of his attitude had helped towards creating a unity near enough complete. Mr. Delcourt stated that, as positions are not clearly defined abroad, it would be wiser to postpone till later the thought of creating a European Union of Karate. Each representative would contact the constituted judo federation in his country and a new meeting would have to take place to create the European Union of Karate. Mr. Delcourt mentioned a certain 'disarray' in existence even in Japan, where about ten different trends are represented. Four members of the FFJAD having been in Japan last summer have brought back complete and detailed information on this point. Apart from the Japan Karate Association in Japan, a new federation has been created which includes a great number of clubs. Mr. Delcourt informed the representatives in attendance at the meeting that he had never contacted Japan, judging that the situation needed to be clarified over there, and thinking that it would be more useful to get organised first at a national basis and then on a European basis. He pointed out that the FFJAD is absolutely independent; it organises its own championship and delivers its own black-belts, recognised by the French government.'

'Mr. Sebban confirmed that the FFJAD would not accept to be subordinated to anyone, but would respect international agreements taken by the managerial committee of the future European Union of Karate. The Italian representative pointed out that the development of karate in his country was slow (difficulties of contact with the judo federations)'.

'Mr. Delcourt specified that at the meeting of the European Union for Judo the question of karate on a European basis certainly would be discussed.'

'Mr. Stas asked that the following rule be created: If official judo federations are not showing interest in karate, it will be permitted to have contacts with the most representative union of the country.'

'Mr. Delcourt proposed to foreign representatives to make all necessary contacts which would allow this desired union to take place within a few months ... and advocated another meeting ... 15th March 1964 at the French Federation.'

'Mr. Regnier declared that because of a great number of experts are called to direct courses, a variety of trends have appeared which does not permit a unification of techniques.'

'Mr. Stas advised not to discuss techniques for the time being, but asked that primarily the rules of refereeing should be defined – the Swiss delegate proposed to exclude beginners from combat.'

'Mr. Caudrelier asked for a stipulation in regulations that strokes given must not be made to full strength, but restrained.'

line 29 – In a letter to Bell dated the 16th April 1964, from Lothar Fischer, we learn that German Karate Association students held the following grades: 1st Dan – 1, 1st kyu – 8, 2nd kyu – 5, 3rd kyu - 12, 4th kyu – 32, and 5th kyu – 57.

Page 276, last line – In a translation of a later undated article in *Budo-Presse,* entitled, 'The Founder of European Karate-Do: Official Interview with Monsieur Henri Plee, 3rd Dan – The Coming of the Japanese Masters,' Plee makes some comments on Harada: 'He was doing normal Shotokan then, not Shotokai. But since he was the personal pupil of Egami, he was extremely interesting. He was a man who performed a Shotokan highly energetically, but [was] limited in the number of techniques. For example, we were doing *oi-zuki* for one hour – but intelligently. He took three men on one side and another three on the other side and he parried and blocked on the right side and left side during a whole hour without interruption. It was an intense and terrible regime. Then we would stop to do a quarter of an hour of blocking and half an hour of *Taikyoku Shodan*! Sometimes a bit of foot work, but not much, for he did not like it. Harada had the quality of having it all in his fists.'

Page 278, line 31 – Bell's uncompromising views of Harada's display are also to be found in a letter to Seydel dated the 28th November. However, Bell acknowledges that Harada was not to blame for what happened. Bell wrote: 'Mr. Harada gave his karate display in London last Saturday, and it was a complete farce ... [because] he performed with a man called Van Donck [*sic*] who ... was worse than any white dog of mine.'

Page 280, line 19 – Between July and December, 1963, Bell employed a thirty year old German, Birgitta Bauer, who was residing in Ilford, to assist him in BKF secretarial work. Bell intended trying to get a publisher for an English version of Seydel's book, *Karate* (1961), and whilst in England, Bauer had translated the first two parts. A number of letters exist between Bell and Bauer after she had returned to Germany, and Bell continued to employ her to translate the third part, which she finished in March 1965. The book was never published in English. Bell described Bauer in a testimonial as 'a conscientious and reliable worker.' After her departure, Bell employed six typists in seven months, one after the other. It would appear that Miss Bauer was hard to replace.

One reference in Bauer's letters is interesting, in that she mentions whether Bell had progressed further with regard to opening his shop. Did Bell plan to open a martial arts' shop? We'll never know, but nothing ever came of the venture.

line 37 – 'Ellwood' should read 'Ellewood.'

Page 285, line 6 – Mochizuki's visit was pre-empted by further correspondence between Bell and Brigitte Chotard, the general secretary of Inter-Activites, based at 54, rue d'Aboukir, Paris 2. The Chotard letters of the 5th and 13th February 1964 have survived, and clarify arrangements. The replies from Bell are lost, and indeed, are unlikely to have been kept.

Training at the London BKF *dojo* under Mochizuki on Friday, 21st February, was between 7.00 p.m. and 9.30 p.m., at a cost of fifteen shillings per student. On Saturday, 22nd February, training times were from 10.00 a.m. to 12.30 p.m., and 2.00 p.m. to 5.00 p.m., at a cost of thirty shillings per pupil. A grading was planned for an hour thereafter, at a cost of five shillings per student, but this never took place. Monies for the lessons were non-returnable, and students were expected to present themselves ten minutes before each lesson.

line 30 – However, Thompson recalled: 'It was a very instructive day. The techniques were different to what we had become used to, but we did not go wild about them … [and that Mochizuki was] a very nice bloke we thought.'

Page 286, line 1 – 'Coatis' should read 'Coates' (and on page 306).

line 3 – Ashton wrote to Bell on the 27th August 1964, and noted that he had taken his 6th kyu under Murakami, in Liverpool, in December 1963.

Paul Cooper and Malcolm Gill, the latter of whom established the BKF Bradford Branch, during kicking practice. INL, 1964 (I/286).

York members practise *shuto-uke* at the INL. Front row, left to right: Keith Stones, John Clark, and Stan Olsen. Back row, left to right: Paul Cooper, Tony Aydon, and Malcolm Gill – 1964 (I/286).

Gordon Thompson and Keith Stones practising *kumite* at the INL – 1964. Note that Stones's kick is likely to be non-specific, as hips were not properly engaged at this time; in other words, the kick is likely to be a hybrid of *keage-geri* and *kekomi-geri* (I/286).

York *dojo* members, 1964/65. Front row, unknown, Patrick O'Donovan, unknown, Steve Cattle, John Clark, Michael O'Donovan (I/286).

Nick Adamou, 1964 (I/301)   Chris Adamou, 1964 (I/301)

line 3 – 'Dearney' should read 'Deamer'(and on page 306).
line 15 – A final letter with regard to the Mochizuki visit comes from J. Commergnat, the treasurer of Inter-Activites, and is dated the 2nd March 1964, concerning four hundred French Francs owed.

Page 287, line 14 – Pauline Bindra (nee Laville), Denise Draper and Janet Revill hold the distinction of being the first women to grade under the BKF, as recorded in the BKF grading register, on the 4th July, 1964. The story of BKF women *karateka* is told in the author's, *You Don't Have to Dress to Kill: Early Female Shotokan Karateka of the British Isles (1957-1966).*

Page 294, line 14 – The 'unknown newspaper' is the *Ilford Pictorial.*

Page 296, photo – (incidental but additional information) Kicks were particularly favoured in photographs because of their unusual and eye-catching nature. In an unknown newspaper of Saturday 2nd January 1965, Tony Aydon of the York *dojo* is shown performing a *yoko-geri* on fellow student, Steve Cattle.

Page 300, line 22 – 'Berrington' should read 'M. Barrington' (and on page 305).
line 34 – According to Bell, Adshead was a Hungarian Artist, and E. Cutting, whom Bell took for private karate lessons, worked for MI5.

line 35 – According to Bell, N. Man worked in publishing.
line 36 – According to Bell, Newman's initial is 'D.'

Page 302, line 22 – An interesting document dated 25th September 1964, shows the requirements for the first four grades of the BKF, now under the auspices of the JKA.

<u>CURRICULUM FOR GRADING EXAMINATION</u>

Hachi-kyu (8th kyu) … white belt

Basic Techniques:
    a) *Zenkutsu-dachi, gedan-gamae* …. M.F [moving forwards]…. *oi-zuki*
    b) *Zenkutsu-dachi* at *hanmi* ….. M.F…. *age-uke*
    c) *Zenkutsu-dachi* at *hanmi* …. .M..F…. *shuto-uke*
    d) *Kokutsu-dachi, shuto-uke* …..M..F…. *shuto-uke*
    e) *Zenkutsu-dachi, gedan-game* …. M.F…. *mae-geri* with rear leg
    f) *Kiba-dachi* …. Crossing legs …. *yoko-geri-keage*
    g) *Kiba-dachi* …. Crossing legs …. *yoko-geri-kekomi*

2. *Kata – Heian* No. 1
3. *Kumite* …. *Gohon-kumite*

Shichi-kyu (7th kyu) … white belt

Basic Techniques
    a) *Zenkutsu-dachi, gedan-gamae* …. M.F …. *oi-zuki*
    b) *Oi-zuki* ….. M.B [moving backwards] …. *age-uke*
    c) *Age-uke* ….. M..F …. *chudan- (soto) ude-uke*
    d) *Ude–uke* ….. M.B …. *kokutsu-dachi, shuto-uke*
    e) *Zenkutsu-dachi, gedan-game* …. M.F …. *mae-geri*
    f) *Kiba-dachi* …. Crossing legs …. *yoko-geri-keage*
    g) *Kiba-dachi* …. Crossing legs …. *yoko-geri-kekomi*

2. *Kata – Heian* No. 2
3. *Kumite* …. *Gohon-kumite*

Roku-kyu (6th kyu) … blue belt

Basic Techniques
    a) *Zenkutsu-dachi, gedan-gamae* …. M.F …. *oi-zuki—sanbon-renzuki*
    b) *Zenkutsu-dachi, gedan-gamae* …. M.B …. *age-uke—gyaku-zuki*
    c) *Gyaku-zuki* ….. M..F…. *chudan- (soto) ude-uke—gyaku-zuki*
    d) *Gyaku-zuk i* ….. M.B…. *kokutsu-dachi, shuto-uke*
    e) *Zenkutsu-dachi, gedan-game* …. M.F…. *mae-geri*
    f) *Kiba-dachi* …. Crossing legs …. *yoko-geri-keage*
    g) *Kiba-dachi* …. Crossing legs …. *yoko-geri-kekomi*

2. *Kata – Heian* No. 3
3. *Kumite …. Kihon-ippon-kumite (choku-zuki* at *jodan* and *chudan,* each twice)

Go-kyu (5th kyu) … purple belt

Basic Techniques
   a) *Zenkutsu-dachi, gedan-gamae ….* M.F…. *oi-zuki—sanbon-renzuki*
   b) *Oi-zuk i…. M.B…. age-uke ….gyaku-zuki*
   c) *Gyaku-zuk i….. M..F…. chudan- (soto) ude-uke—gyaku-zuki*
   d) *Gyaku-zuk i ….. M.B…. kokutsu-dachi, shuto-uke—zenkutsu-dachi,nukite*
   e) *Zenkutsu-dachi, gedan-game ….* M.F…. *mae-geri—ren-geri* at *chudan* and *jodan*
   f) *Kiba-dachi ….* Crossing legs …. *yoko-geri-keage—yoko-geri-kekomi*
   g) *Zenkutsu-dachi ….* M.F…. *mawashi-geri*

2. *Kata – Heian* No. 4
3. *Kumite …. Kihon-ippon-kumite (choku-zuki at jodan and chudan, each twice)*

Page 305 – 'Barrett' should read 'Barnett.'

Page 306 – 'Brayant' should read 'Bryant.'

Page 310 – remove '223' as the first entry for Roebuck
            – add '109' as the first page entry for Sen.

ADDITIONS TO VOL. II OF *SHOTOKAN DAWN*

Page 21, line 14 – In a translation of a later, undated article in *Budo-Presse,* entitled, 'The Founder of European Karate-Do: Official Interview with Monsieur Henri Plee, 3rd Dan – The Coming of the Japanese Masters,' Plee makes some comments on Ohshima: 'When he arrived, I realised his style was more than interesting … it was 'pure.' I told myself, 'I can not see anybody doing better than Ohshima.' He stayed in France no more than fifteen days the first time. But a year later, he came back with his wife for one year. He made a [financial] sacrifice by it, I believe.'

Page 27, photograph – On the front cover of the Christmas card is a picture of a samurai.

Page 30, line 32 – In a later, undated three-page letter/memo to unknown persons, Bell wrote on page 2: 'He [Kazuo Nagai] … informed us that as of 1964, the Yoseikan was now a large member club of the Japan Karate Association, and all grades conferred by the Yoseikan had to be ratified and nationally re-registered with the Japan Karate Association in Tokyo. Because of this, I was awarded and registered as a *Shodan* of the JKA, which would then be an internationally recognised grade from the official body in Japan, recognised by the Japanese Ministry of Education.'

Page 34, line 22 – In a letter to Seydel dated the 25th April 1964, Bell gave his impressions of Tat-Man: 'He is very intelligent and extremely polite, and a gentle man of high integrity, and I found him very sincere.'

Page 35, photograph (top) – An accompanying translation to Bell's *Shodan* certificate, signed by Nakayama and Masutani [this is the generally accepted method of writing this name {Masuya is recorded in *Shotokan Dawn* as per the JKA correspondence}], reads: 'Mr. V.C.F. Bell is hereby licensed to rank in the *Shodan* grade of karate, in recognition of the great progress that he has made by his diligent study of the art. We expect him to endeavor for further progress in the future.'

    photograph (bottom) – An accompanying translation of the affiliation certificate, signed by Masutani, reads: 'I, the undersigned, certify that the British Karate Federation has been recognised as an exclusive representative of the Japan Karate Association for the territories of England, Wales, Scotland, Northern Ireland, Channel and Icelus [*sic*], in accordance with the rules and regulations set forth by the Japan Karate Association, and has been registered as such in the official book. The British Karate Federation is requested to devote itself for the development of the true art of karate in co-operation with its principal.'

Page 36, line 23 – Habura's first name is John (from an undated {though 1964}, handwritten letter to Bell); in fact, it is Habura Jnr. This letter also invites Habura to attend a meeting in Paris on behalf of the BKF from the 23rd-25th of an unknown month, to which Habura replied that he was honoured to be asked, but was unable to attend due to work commitments. There are actually two handwritten letters from Habura that have survived – the second, also undated, provides Habura's Forces' address.

Page 39, line 7 – The three Japanese were Wado-ryu seniors, Tatsuo Suzuki, 5th Dan, Toru Arakawa, 5th Dan, and Takashima, 4th Dan, visiting on behalf of the Zen Nippon Karate Renmei, of Japan. The British Kendo Association held the demonstration of 'Karate and Kendo-*no-kata*' at the Shinto-Ryu Kendo Dojo and London Judo Society, at 32, St. Oswald's Place, London, S.E. 11. The demonstration commenced at 7.30 p.m. The Japanese were on a two-month (April and May) tour of Europe and the U.S.A, initially at the invitation of the Danish Government. Their visit was arranged through Takizawa Kozo, 7th Dan, Honorary President of the BKA, who lived in Japan. Literature from the BKA in relation to the planned event noted: 'Karate is in a difficult stage in this country at the present time, and it is hoped that the visit of three such reputable masters to present an official demonstration on the premises of one of the leading judo clubs, the London Judo Society, in this Kendo *dojo*, will help the development of this art in the future.' The demonstration was featured in *Judo* magazine article, entitled, simply, 'Karate' (Vol. 8, No. 10, July 1964, pp. 37-38). The article notes that Knutsen, a 3rd Dan in Kendo, organised the special programme, and that representatives from the BBC, British Judo Association and Ministry of Education, were present. Suzuki, as leader of the group, explained the basic moves of karate through an interpreter, Miss Etsuko Horie, and then followed, 'a fascinating exhibition of lightning like moves of hands and feet [that] mesmerised the audience ... the accuracy of their blows was a frightening experience for the spectators.' Both wood and, unusually, stone were broken in the display, and 'here the select audience saw a remarkable performance.' Five photographs accompanied the article.

Page 41, line 1 – Michael Benson applied for membership to the BKF on the 8th August 1963, aged twenty-four, and a local government officer by occupation. He accepted the position of Area Officer for the BKF in a letter to Bell dated the 5th September 1963. A feasibility meeting was held at Maindee Primary School, Newport, of the 13th March 1964, with a view to establish a Newport BKF *dojo*. Benson applied to the BKF with this proposal on the 8th June, but resigned in November from 'extreme annoyance' with Bell. William Moore took over the job of club secretary, but in a letter to Bell dated the 7th January 1965, noted that: 'The club never held one training session.' The last letter from considerable correspondence to have survived between Benson/Moore and Bell in dated the 21st January 1965, when Moore noted the club intended joining Master Harada and the BKC. The whole saga of the BKF Newport *dojo* appears to have been a rather unhappy affair. Members of the club were: James Foley, 29, carpenter (3.6.64); Anthony Harrison, 25, bricklayer (4.3.64); Edward Mahagan, 33, foundry machine operator (19.3.64); Alan Moore, 28, carpenter (16.4.64); William Moore, 30, motor fitter (14.3.64); Colin Viner, 21, steelworker (30.4.64); William Viner, 21, foundry worker (16.4.64); Malcolm White, 22, foundry worker (16.3.64).

Page 45, line 27 – Nicol did indeed know of Bell's existence. In the *BKF Register of Enquiries*, entry twenty-five contains a C.W. Nicol of Gilchrist Avenue, Cheltenham, who was a 5th kyu of Cheltenham Judo Club. Under 'Reason of Enquiry' is written, 'To join the BKF.' A letter of reply was sent on the 10th February 1959. Nicol acknowledged this letter on the 25th August 1959; the delay being to 'On Canadian expedition —- [word unclear] on return home.'

A Christmas card sent from Takagi to Bell (II/50)

In his introductory letter to Bell, from Japan, dated the 29th November 1964, Nicol, on the reverse side of the Aerogramme letter, wrote, as a postscript: 'If you look into your records for 1959, you may well find my name – formerly of the Cheltenham Judo Club. I couldn't afford to study karate in England as a student.' Nicol's address in Tokyo was: 1538 3-chome Aoba-cho, Higashi Murayama Shin.

Page 47, line 24 – 'Tatsu' should read 'Tatsuo.'

Page 48, line 37 – Kanazawa referred to Nicol's encouragement to come to England in *Kanazawa, 10th Dan* ... On page 186, Kanazawa noted, 'Nicol *San* was enthusiastic about the idea and explained all about Great Britain to me.'

Page 52, line 3 – This telegram was sent in reply to one sent by the JKA of the same date. The JKA telegram read: 'KANAZAWA LEAVING TOKYO TWENTY-SEVENTH PLEASE PAY AIRFARE BOAC LONDON URGENTLY CONFIRM.'

Page 54, line 7 – Newly discovered correspondence between Bell and Surgeon Captain H.G. Silvester, Chairman of the Plymouth Command Judo Club, shows that a civil misunderstanding took place over financial reimbursement for the expenses incurred by the BKF.

Page 55, line 3 – In an undated letter to Bell, we learn from Takagi that, 'Mr. Kanazawa and the other three instructors left Japan [on an overnight flight] on February 27th as scheduled.' Attached to this previously lost letter is an itinerary, details of which are given on the next few pages.

line 13 – The party spent twelve days on Hawaii, arriving on the 28th February and departing on the 10th March.

line 27 – The party spent four days in Los Angeles, arriving on the 10th March and departing on the 14th March. The party then spent two days in San Francisco, arriving on the 14th March and departing on [an overnight flight] on the 16th March.

line 28 – The party then spent ten days in Chicago, arriving on the 17th March and departing on the 27th March.

line 29 – The party then appears to have spent six days in Philadelphia and New York, arriving on the 27th March and departing on the 2nd April.

Page 56, photograph caption – caption should read 'From left to right.'

line 4 – The JKA party's itinerary notes that they had planned to arrive in Germany on the 3rd April.

line 20 – The JKA party's itinerary notes that after Germany, they had planned to fly to Zurich on the 10th April, and over the next twelve days visit Paris, Belgium and Amsterdam, before flying to London on the 22nd April.

Page 57, line 1 – C. Goetz's card, which was orange, shows that he and fellow instructor J. Dehaes, both students of Tsutomu Ohshima, who had taught in Europe for just under one year before returning to California, had their *dojo* at 182, rue Royale, Bruxelles 1.

(A Bernhard Goetz, the national coach for the German Karate Federation, visited the Blackfriars *dojo* sometime before March 1967. Goetz had trained at the JKA from 1963 to 1966, but the article by John Goodbody in *Karate News* (March), makes it unclear whether he was a *Shodan* or *Nidan*. The Belgium Goetz and the German Goetz should not be confused).

Page 58, line 2 – On page 187 of the author's, *Kanazawa, 10th Dan: Recollections of a Living Karate Legend – The Early Years (1931-*

1964) (Shoto Publishing, 2001), Kanazawa recalled being met at the airport: 'When I went to England, only Vernon Bell and two students were at Heathrow.' This experience was in direct contrast to when the master landed in Hawaii in January 1961, where, 'There were quite a few people [about thirty] waiting to greet me' (p. 146). The two students who met Kanazawa are believed to have been Wingrove and Neal.

Page 59, line 20 – 91, Perryman's Farm Road became the administrative address of the BKF, Bell's British Jujitsu Federation and the National Judo Association of Great Britain, from the 1st December 1963.

Page 63, line 19 – In an undated (though likely to be 1964, and certainly no later than 1966) document entitled, 'Nihon Karate Kyokai, Inc. Japanese Karate Association: Register of Names,' come some interesting facts. The first eleven pages of this document, printed as a fifteen-page booklet, lists the JKA clubs in Japan, in Japanese. The last four pages, however, list 'Overseas Member Organizations,' in English. For comparative purposes, these will be given below, in abbreviated form, using the format of: country, association name, location of contact (if not obvious), name of contact, so:

USA – All American Karate Federation, Inc., Los Angeles: Thomas McCarthy & Hidetaka Nishiyama
 – Kansas Karate Association: Wayne Noell
 – Karate Association of Hawaii, Honolulu: Masataka Mori
 – East Coast Karate Association: i) Philadelphia: Teruyuki Okazaki; ii) New York: Hiroshi Orito & Herman Kauz
 – Colorado Karate Association, Denver: Joseph Castillo
 – The Karate Association of Chicago: Wataru Nakamoto & Shojiro Sugiyama
 – Florida Karate Association: i) Tampa: Clippard L. Salter, Richard Herdiman; ii) Lakeland: David Kaufman & Donald McNatt; iii) Homestead: Penny Hutson; iv) Homes Beach: Gree Golden
 – Twin City School of Karate, Minneapolis: Robert Fusaro
 – Santa Ana Karate School: Daniel Ivan
 – Louisiana Karate Association, New Orleans: Douglas Abadie
 – U.S. Armed Forces Karate Association, Colorado Springs: Harry Danntsuka,
 – Alabama Karate Association, Mobile: Dr. Joseph Miller
Canada – Canadian Federation of Karate, St. Laurent: Ary Anastasiadis
Belgium   – Belgische Nationale Karate Federation, Antwerp: Leo Aarts
  – Ecole Europeanne De Karate Japonais, Bruxelles: J. Dehaes & C. Goetz
Great Britain – The British Karate Federation: Vernon Bell
Germany – Deutscher Karate Bunde V., Brucknerallee: Lothar Fischer
Ireland – The Irish Karate-Do Society, Dublin: A. Ruddock & H. [*sic*] Robinson
South Africa – The Japan Karate Association of Transvall, Extension 2: James Rousseau

 – The Japan Karate Association of Natal, Durban: Geo Higginson
 – The Japan Karate Association of East Transvall, Johannesburg: Stan Schmidt
 – The Japan Karate Association of Cape Town: John Thomson
Philippines – Seiken Karate-Do Association, Bacalod City Neg.: Pedro Jose Unson
Malaya – Malaya Karate Club, Seremban: Thamby Rajah
New Zealand – New Zealand Karate Association, Te Atatu, Auckland : P. Lee
Australia – Australia Karate Association: H. Steele
Yugoslavia – Zagreb: Zarko Modric
Venezuela – Caracas: Francisco Forero
Iran – Teheran: Sirus Jahanshaki
Turkey – Ankars: Riza Dogan
Brazil   – Brazil Karate Association: i) Rio de Janeiro: Sadami Uriu; ii) Sao Paulo: Juichi Sagara & Tetsuma Higashino
United Arab Republic – Cairo: El Sayed M. Kandil
Indonesia – Indonesia Karate Association, Djakarta: Baud Adikusumo

line 22 – In a letter to McGuire dated the 1st June 1965, we learn from Bell that the *dojo* was costing ten guineas in rent per week.

Page 71, photograph – Gordon Thompson still has a broken board, signed by the Japanese instructors hanging up in his lounge 'ever since Neil MacDonald brought it back for me from the course.'

Page 73, line 32 – Another article on the Hornsey demonstration appeared on page 2 of the *North London Press* (Islington Edition) on Friday, 30th April 1965, by an unknown reporter. The three accompanying photographs show Master Enoeda breaking a wooden board from three angles, with a punch (these photographs appear in the author's, *Kanazawa Years ...,* page 60). The piece, entitled, 'Japs Impress With 'Empty-Hand Fighting,' describes the 'spectacular effects' of the Japanese display, and goes on to mention that the masters demonstrated the main *kata*, and that 'Members of the British Karate Federation under Terry Wingrove (2nd kyu) showed basic training methods.'

Page 78 – The date of the photograph has been confirmed in a letter from Bell to J. Ashton, who served on the Liverpool BKF Committee.

Page 79, line 2 – Correspondence at the time from Ashton to Bell shows that Granada Television would have preferred 'live' coverage if a camera crew was available. Presumably they weren't available, and hence the studio appointment 'one afternoon.' Final arrangements with the television company had to be made by the 15th April 1965, and in

Master Kanazawa looks on as brown-belt Jimmy Neal pairs-up with Mick Peachey at the St. Mary's *dojo* – May-July, 1965 (II/83).

a letter to Ashton, Bell noted that the TV demonstration would be best in the afternoon of the 23rd – before the trip to Liverpool and the St. George's Hall display in the evening.

line 4 – The London, Liverpool and Blackpool *dojos* appear to have shared the travel costs of Bell and the four Japanese.

line 30 – According to the JKA party's itinerary, the three JKA instructors had planned to fly out to Johannesburg on the 28th April.

Page 84, line 18 – Bell booked Kanazawa's First Class return ticket from Euston to Liverpool at a cost of £4-1-0.

Jack Green – BKF Blackpool *dojo,* 1963 (II/85)

Page 86, line 35 – Ralph Andersen, 17, schoolboy (17.3.65); Paterson Barnes, 32, bus driver (9.10.64); Brian Bennett, 26, clerk (16.10.64); Raymond Boag, 20, apprentice engineer (15.5.64); James Brady, 18, labourer (10.10.64); Hugh Brown, 17, schoolboy (27.3.65); William Budge, 18, student (22.1.65); Ronald Burns, 18, apprentice glazier (28.5.64); William Burns, 21, line operator (28.4.64); Robert Carsewell, 17, steel worker (-.-.66); James Cochrane, 19, apprentice electrician (6.9.64); Alexander Craigie, 33, labourer (28.3.65); Alfred Craik, 32, electrician (22.5.65); David Crane, 32, project engineer (10.8.64); David Danks, 20, journalist (10.10.64); James Dye, 27, labourer (27.3.65); Frank Elder, 17, apprentice civil engineer (18.4.65); Stewart Ellis, 19, apprentice toolmaker (29.5.64); John Flynn, 26, labourer (27.3.65); Andrew Forbes, 25, process engraver (-.-.64); John Frearson, 20, student (18.4.65); John Gall, 22, student (-.-.65); Norman Gowans, 23, photo engraver (11.3.65); Lewis Greig, 19, apprentice engineer (24.6.64); Anthony Grilli, 22, shop assistant (29.3.65); Ronald Hare, 17, apprentice electrician (-.-.65); Brian Hogg, 19, apprentice electrician (23.10.64); John Huband, 23, salesman (18.5.65); John Hughes, 17, mechanical engineer (29.3.65); Alastair Lindsay, 23, machine operator (27.2.65); Allan Lobban, 29, watch analyst (-.-.65). Other students are mentioned in correspondence for whom membership forms do not survive, though they almost certainly belonged to the BKF, having paid monies. Information on these individuals is sketchy, but their ages at the time of training, occupation and year of entry, if known, will be provided. They are: T. Bamburgh (1965); Ian Cassidy (1964); J. Frinney (1965); H. Gowers (1965); S. Hill (1965); A. Lowden (1964); D. Nolan, 23, bus driver (1965); Alexander Phinn (1964); Anthony Quinn (1964); Frank Rodgers, 45 (1965); Malcolm Steadman (or Steedman), assistant storeman (1964); J. Stubbs (1965); H. Thomson. Individuals who may have been members (though do not appear in later analyses in this book) are: J. Ashton (1965); Charles Fitchet (1965); C. Hill (1965); Ian McFee, 15; D. Russell, 20, hopperman (1965); James Samson, 19, plumber (1964); G. Tierney, 25, boatman (1965). The names Durrall, Gansh, McMahon and Robertson also appear.

The BKF Dundee correspondence is considerable and mostly administrative, and only salient points, treated as a block unit, will be entered into here. The full title of the club was, in fact, the South Angus and Dundee Branch. In the earliest letter to have survived referring to the branch, Bell replies to a Mr. J. Whittet, a judo *Shodan* of the BJC, who was, apparently, studying karate, on the 13th May 1964. In this explanative, three-and-a-half page letter, we learn that McGuire, who had not yet secured a *dojo*, was appointed the BKF local officer for Dundee in February that year. Because of interfering forces, Bell noted that McGuire had resigned his position, but continued, in a postscript, that he now wished to be re-instated and had secured a *dojo*.

The first letter to survive from McGuire is dated the 8th June 1964, and is administrative, but in another letter to Bell dated the 25th June, we learn that McGuire was training twice weekly and keeping 'strictly to the syllabus – and only the first *Pinan kata*.' In a later, undated letter (probably late June/early July 1964), and from numerous others, we see that McGuire was very keen and had a carpenter make a striking post (in a later letter dated the 9th August, we find that this 'striking post' was six feet tall and padded in three places). This enthusiasm was obviously contagious, for Bell spent considerable time writing out the first two *Heian kata* for him.

McGuire applied for club affiliation to the BKF in the letter of the 9th August 1964, and in another letter of that date, we learn that training was on Wednesdays and Fridays, between 7.00 p.m. and 8.00. p.m. In a letter to Bell dated the 3rd September, we learn that McGuire was trying to procure larger premises and intended, on Bell's advice, to have longer training hours.

In McGuire's letter to Bell dated the 6th September, we learn that he travelled down to Essex and trained with Wingrove and Neal.

McGuire ran a very tight ship, and commented on a case that, whilst showing his obvious enthusiasm for correctness, might seem ludicrous today. In a letter to Bell dated the 19th September 1964, McGuire wrote: 'Mister Smith has decided that he wishes to back out. He says that he has a traffic offence coming to court shortly, and he will have damages, plus a fine, and other expenses to pay. I told him that we could not take anybody that had any police offences.' In a reply letter dated the 23rd September, Bell noted: 'Regards Mr. Smith, I think you are a little too strict in refusing his admittance to the branch, for he is only guilty of a traffic offence, which is not really a criminal offence, so I will suggest you reconsider his application, for we cannot refuse good members on trivial traffic offences, especially when the man has been honest. I, too, have a traffic offence in court at the end of this month for speeding, but I don't think the BKF would expel me. So, we will proceed with his membership ...'

In a letter to Bell dated the 14th November 1964, McGuire wrote: 'I have had quite a few ladies asking if they could enrol with the BKF ... and also if I can enrol anyone under sixteen years.' In an undated reply, Bell noted: 'Regards the ladies enrolling in the BKF, this is quite permissible ... with a proviso that they will train separately as a group under you, but on the same system and methods, excepting in a much softer manner. Their fees will be the same. Regards applicants under sixteen years, we accept those over fourteen only, providing you get a letter from the parent accepting full responsibility ...'

A certain dissatisfaction, to put it mildly, had set in following a meeting, as McGuire's letter to Bell on the 28th February 1965, clearly shows. McGuire wrote: 'I had the impression at the conference that neither you, nor your instructor, Mr. Wingrove, were interested in us in Scotland. If this is so, just let me know in your reply and you will hear no more from me, nor our branch. I assure you we will have no difficulty in finding another organisation who are interested. I think you will admit I have worked very hard to uphold the BKF. We in Dundee need some help. We have never had a course from you, or any of your instructors, because we have never been able to pay the expenses required by you. Please let me know by return what your decision is regarding the points I mention, as our members here await your reply with interest. I must point out that they are unanimous in their decision to leave the BKF if we are to be ignored any longer. If you feel that you can send Mr. Kanazawa for a week [in the future, for Kanazawa had not yet arrived], then he will have to come alone, as we cannot afford any extra expense of anyone else.'

Bell's response came on the 2nd March 1965, in the form of a four-and-a-half page letter. Bell wrote that he was 'extremely surprised and very upset at the contents of this letter and, to say the least, am most displeased, but you are perfectly entitled to speak your mind, and it may be better to bring these things into the open.' Bell appreciated the problems that McGuire faced so far from London and was most reasonable, offering him the three Japanese (Kase, Enoeda and Shirai) at minimal expense, and even offering him a weekend course free-of-charge under himself, if he paid for his (and his children's) expenses. McGuire's reply came on the 9th March, and all was well again between the two men.

McGuire's letter of the 9th March 1965, gives rise to an objectionable, and the author might say, prophetic point. McGuire noted that whilst he respected Bell, he could not say the same for some others at a BKF meeting. McGuire wrote: 'I thought that a conference should always be a serious discussion of past and present activities, and also future plans. How is it possible to do this when you have people behind you pulling all sorts of jokes like handfuls of rice, as if it were animals you were talking about. At the same time, another two [were] bantering to each other about haggis growing on trees – all this mind while you were talking. If I want to hear this kind of talk, I don't have to travel four hundred miles.' Bell replied to this letter on the 15th March: 'I quite agree with you that some behave like imbeciles, but it is better to ignore them.'

Members of the Dundee club were renovating their new *dojo* at Dudhope Castle (a previous *dojo* being based at the Masonic Halls, Artillery Lane), and training was four times a week – Monday, Wednesday, Friday and Sunday. In the meanwhile, McGuire was unable to secure a large hall for the Japanese and had to cancel the intended visit. McGuire also mentions a film that Bell had, which he leant to him, entitled, 'Self Defence,' by Kanazawa (and in a later letter by Bell, dated the 6th April, this film is again referred to). McGuire, at this time, was 8th kyu.

A letter to McGuire, dated the 30th March 1965, shows how much work Bell was putting into the arrival and promotion of the four Japanese, placing aside all other BKF business. By the 1st June, Bell wrote to McGuire: 'I am so hard pressed with work, which is increasing, that I am now working round the clock and engaging staff to help me...'

McGuire was featured on page 8 of the *Sunday Post* on the 9th May 1965, in a light-hearted but informative article entitled: 'Ssh! HON

Learns A Deadly Secret – Uncanny Experience with the Karate Boys,' by an unknown reporter. In Bell's 1st June letter, we know that he found the article, 'very interesting and quite readable, but I was rather disappointed and surprised that no mention was made of your own executive status, nor of your branch affiliation with the BKF …'

Bell replied on the 6th July 1965 to a lost letter from McGuire, who was evidently having difficulties financing a planned visit from Kanazawa. Bell had little sympathy with McGuire on this point, commenting: 'We feel that the fault is not ours in the Federation, and your argument that there is too much money required for courses is erroneous, for you have as many members in your branch as any of the other branches, and as Area Officer you should clearly indicate to them that if they want qualified, high-grade instruction, they must be prepared to assist economically in the expenses involved for the development of their branch. If they are not prepared to put their hands in their pockets and pay one pound each for a week's course from high-grade instruction, which from the members on your file would cover Mr. Kanazawa's twenty-five pounds a week, plus his keep, and this your members should fully realise, if they don't [agree], they are not true karate men, and neither are they worth bothering about.'

Following a dispute at the Dundee branch, an extraordinary general meeting was held on Sunday, 18th July, at Dudhope Castle. Complaints were raised by a number of members about the allegedly authoritarian manner in which McGuire was running the *dojo*. The report of the meeting noted: 'McGuire stated that too often the trouble has been that too many members were not bothering and that he had to have some form of discipline.' A motion of no confidence in McGuire was carried by eighteen votes to eight and it was proposed that he should resign. Initially not accepting the decision, McGuire 'later wrote a letter of resignation, signed by himself and witnessed by club members. He also signed over the keys of the *dojo*.' Though in a letter dated the 20th July by a student whose signature is unclear, though whose first name is 'John' [there are five known Dundee Branch members with the Christian name 'John'], we learn that McGuire returned the next day 'to change the padlock' to the *dojo*.

This meeting caused a flurry of letters from McGuire and Dundee committee members to Bell over the next few days, and it is not the intention of the author to get drawn into this debate. However, in an undated letter by Stables to Bell, we learn that Kanazawa did visit the club for a weekend and that 'the absolute chaos that attended Mr. Kanazawa's visit was due to the fact that no one knew he was coming' (undated letter to Bell by 'John'). and 'only six of us could attend' (letter to Bell, by Danks, 21st July).

Things did not clear themselves up and Stables wrote to Bell on the 27th July, noting that members 'intend to start up a club on our own,' and requested BKF blessing. In a letter dated the 10th August, Bell wrote to an unknown individual noting that: 'This is to certify that Mr. W. McGuire of 22, St. Peter's Street, Dundee, is the ONLY duly appointed representative and Area Officer for Dundee of this Federation, and only he is our authorised agent for Dundee to carry out the development of karate for your area as a duly elected officer of this Federation … NO individual member or group of members of the BKF can either demand his resignation or force him from his position in the branch. Mister McGuire enjoys the full confidence and support of the National Federation.' A similar letter, backing McGuire, was sent by Bell to the manager of the Dundee Savings Bank the same day. So, it is quite clear on which side Bell's camp was sited.

On the 19th August, Bell received a letter from Drummond, Johnstone and Grosset, writers, on behalf of a student and several other members, 'who are anxious to know how they stand in relation to the Branch and also the Federation.' Bell sent a copy of this letter to McGuire (letter to Bell from Drummond, Johnstone and Grosset, dated the 26th August). Bell wrote to the solicitors on the 26th August: 'With reference to your letter of the 19th instant, we wish to point out that we have no desire to enter any correspondence with outside bodies upon any matters pertaining to the internal policy of the BKF. We would also add that the persons referred to in your letter [no persons were actually referred to] are now no longer members of the BKF, and we now regard the entire matter as closed.' A letter from the solicitors dated the 30th August shows that they didn't necessarily agree that their clients were no longer BKF members. The final letter to have survived on this incident was a letter sent by Bell on the 7th September, informing the solicitors that the Dundee Branch of the BKF was no longer functioning, Bell concluding, 'I will be glad if you will not pester me any further with the matter you raised, for I have no intention of having any further relationship with the people concerned.'

McGuire wrote to Bell on the 5th September noting, 'I have been granted direct affiliation to [the] Japan Karate Association at a meeting of the board of directors in Tokyo. This was granted on a strong recommendation from Mr. Kanazawa. My certificate has been sent, and I am sure you will extend me your best wishes in this enterprise.' Bell replied on the 21st September, none too happy, commenting that he had read McGuire's and the 'rebels'' letters at the Area Officer meeting, 'which were discussed fully, and we feel that this is burnt ground now and the whole thing stinks to high heaven and we have no further wish to discuss it.' Bell continued that, 'I feel I was sold a dummy in all your troubles and I stuck my neck out to help you and quite frankly it is most unrewarding and best forgotten.' McGuire had hoped that Kanazawa would soon be up in Dundee again to teach his (at the time) seventeen members. Kanazawa was under contract to Bell, and Bell informed McGuire as such, and that Kanazawa would not be coming to Dundee, noting that 'this is one of the misfortunes that occur when people decide to go it alone.' The last letter to have survived between the two men is from McGuire, dated the 20th June 1966, concerning finances.

Page 88, last line – A number of requests came from non-BKF *karateka* wishing to train under Kanazawa at the London *dojo*. Most noteworthy perhaps were two German enquiries. The first of these requests came in a letter dated the 29th June 1965, from 1st kyu, Karl Grosche, who wished to train with Kanazawa when visiting London for a few days, after seeing Kase, Kanazawa, Enoeda and Shirai's demonstration in the spring that year in Bad Godesberg. Bell replied on the 6th July welcoming Grosche at no charge, as he did to Werner Bode (see Vol. I), who wrote to Bell on the 16th July 1965, asking if he and other German students (from 3rd kyu to *Shodan*) could come and train. Once again, Bell replied (on the 20th July), inviting them to do so. In a later letter to Lothar Fischer, Vice-President of the German Karate Federation, Bell noted that Bode, Peter Schmidt and Manfred Ruhnke, would be coming to Britain to train. The author is unaware, however, as to whether or not they attended.

Bell had a sound and confidential relationship with the German Karate Federation, and an issue arose to show how good relationships were. In a letter dated the 27th July 1965, Fischer asked Bell whether 'it would be possible for you and your organisation to give Mr. Kanazawa a short leave for a visit to Germany.' In Bell's reply letter of the 10th August, we learn, surprisingly, that, 'I have discussed with Mr. Kanazawa the prospect of visiting Germany later this year and he is pleased and happy to do so. Our Federation is quite willing to release him from his contract and give him leave to visit Germany for an eight day course.' This must be considered a most generous gift from Bell. However, as far as the author is aware, Kanazawa did not visit Germany at this time.

Patrick O'Donovan sings an Irish song as Ian MacLaren plays guitar and Steve Cattle looks on – July, 1965 (II/91).

The INL Working Men's Club in 2002. Kanazawa taught at this *dojo*, the floor of which was slippery, on his first trip to York in 1965. Thompson recalled: 'While we had to change in the hall itself, I managed to arrange for Kanazawa to have the use of the artiste's changing room, the one they used when they put on concerts and the like and I think he much appreciated this. The disapproving elements [of the INL] showed the worst possible manners. They understood the situation, but half-way through the training one night they exercised their right as members to come into the hall bringing their wives with them. I think Kanazawa understood the situation as he put up with it with remarkable tolerance. Only once was he led to exclaim to them, 'Please be quiet'' (II/95).

Page 93, line 3 – A caption from a photograph of January 1965, notes that training at the INL club was twice weekly (which we learn from a clipping from an unknown newspaper was Tuesdays and Wednesdays). The number of training evenings were increased in York when Kanazawa was teaching.

Page 96, line 3 – Anthony Aydon went on to reach *Nidan*; John Clark, *Shodan* (in 1967/68).

Page 97, line 2 – Burgess's initial is 'J,' Elgie's initial is 'V,' Hall's initial is 'B.'

     line 3 – Hepworth's initial is 'D' (and 'Hepworth, P.' should be removed from page 201).

     line 6 – 'Redman' should read 'Redfern' (and on page 203).

Master Kanazawa aboard Thompson's yacht – 1965 (II/96)

line 7 – Hagon's, Hart's and Shaw's initials are 'D,' 'D' and 'I,' respectively.

last line – The list of Rotherham BKF students has been discovered. The club was formed by Brinsworth Judo Club member, Kenneth Roebuck, who applied for membership of the BKF in March 1964, when aged twenty-three, and a joiner by trade. Members details are as follows: Malcolm Allen, 21, bricklayer (28.1.66); Rex Best, 18, apprentice plater (11.3.65); John Boughen, 22, welder (15.3.65); John

Burgess, 20, plumber (19.1.65); Robert Burgess, 23, sheet metal worker (19.2.65); David Culyer, 18, coalface worker (-.-.64); Stuart Davies, 26, bricklayer (29.9.65); Vernon Elgie, 19, plater (15.3.65); Michael Flanagan, 17, cellar man (26.9.65); Brian Fletcher, 30, local government officer (8.2.66); Brian Glave, 30, welder (-.-.65); Dennis Hagon, 25, fitter's mate (21.5.64); William Hagon, 22, bricklayer (26.1.66); Brian Hall, 26, grinder (14.6.65); Michael Harper, 17, trainee representative (11.9.65); David Hart, 20, painter/decorator (22.5.64); David Hepworth, 18, schoolboy (20.5.65); David Holroyd, 19, apprentice joiner (-.-.66); Walter Howarth, 21, miner (30.12.64); Eric Kaye, 23, joiner (4.11.64); John King, 23, clerk (20.6.65); David Mellard, 15, schoolboy (29.1.65); Paul Mellard, 17, engineer (15.3.65); James Mower, 23, joiner (24.1.66); John Mulliss, 23, waiter (21.10.65); Ernest Oades, 23, insurance agent (22.12.64); Michael O'Keefe, 25, pipe fitter's mate (28.6.65); John Ramsden, 17, fireman (19.2.65); Austin Redfern, 36, sales representative (10.7.65); Keith Royston, 25, joiner (21.10.65); Keith Sayles, 21, painter (22.5.64); Ian Shaw, 19, apprentice joiner (19.5.64); George Shettler, 18, weaver (15.3.65); Peter Swift, 21, student surveyor (21.10.65); Albert Tinsley, 24, back man [?] (20.10.65); Reginald Wharton, 21, laboratory technician (5.1.65). A Mr. Vale, who graded to 7th kyu, is also mentioned in a letter from Roebuck to Bell dated the 24th November 1965.

The correspondence to have survived between members of the Rotherham club and Bell is considerable, and raises some valuable information. The first Bell knew of interest in karate in Rotherham was in an undated (but March 1964) letter from Roebuck. Roebuck's enthusiasm shines through, not only in this letter, but also in many subsequent ones. He wrote: 'I am tremendously interested in karate and have been practising privately every day for about two years now. I am entirely self-taught from the well-known books on the subject, such as, *Karate...* by Nishiyama and Brown, *The Way of Karate*, by George Mattson, and, *What is Karate*, by Oyama. I have reached a fair standard in kicks, strikes, blocks and combination techniques. I also perform, reasonably well, the *Ei-an [Heian] Shodan kata*.

'About a year ago, I endeavoured to teach some close friends what I had learned of the art, and I am pleased to say that we now have a small, but very keen group practising together twice a week. I hasten to say that we are all of good character and are studying seriously with the highest possible motives.

'I have only just become aware of the British Judo [should read 'Karate'] Federation, otherwise you would have been pestered by me

Ken Roebuck – BKF Rotherham *dojo*, 1964

a long time ago.

'I wonder if you could let me have the address of the nearest karate club to me, or if there is not one near, perhaps the address of your nearest member.

'If it is at all possible, I would be deeply grateful and honoured if I could be permitted to join your movement.'

Bell replied to Roebuck's letter of the 19th March 1964, and this was followed by a letter from Jack Hancock, a Further Education Organiser from the Education Office of the County Borough of Rotherham. Hancock wrote: 'I have been approached recently by a group of young men who, besides attending official judo classes, are pursuing the study of classical karate in their own homes. They now find these circumstances somewhat confining and are seeking accommodation from this Authority in order to have better facilities for their activities. As I have but a minimum of information concerning karate, I should be grateful for some guidance from your Federation, in order to have a more comprehensive picture. I gather from various local sources, none of them authoritative, that there is some difficulty in providing instructors for karate because of the danger attached to this subject. You can see, therefore, that I feel it is imperative to have full information before I am able to assist this very enthusiastic local group.'

Bell always responded well to such letters, and replied on the 23rd March sending BKF details, noting that the purpose of the BKF was to 'teach karate as a system for physical education, mental and physical co-ordination, and a highly competitive sport developed on a World basis in co-operation with the education authorities in each country.'

Bell replied to an undated and now lost letter by Roebuck on the 13th May. Bell advised Roebuck to go and call on Mr. Hancock as nothing had been heard, but noted: 'Meanwhile, you will be well advised to continue your practice in your rented hall, for it is BKF general policy for all our branches to be self-supporting and completely independent of all authoritative organisations not associated with karate, even though we welcome their help and liaison. I suggest that you now enrol your five members as Associates into the Federation without delay. With yourself already in this [Federation], [this] makes six, which qualifies your group for official affiliation.'

A letter from Roebuck to Bell dated the 31st May, noted Hancock 'feels that he cannot help us. He pointed out that although I am Branch Officer for the BKF, I as yet hold no grade, and a ruling of the education committee is that an unqualified person is not allowed to teach a class on any subject. However, I agree with you that it is better for us to be a completely self-supporting branch.'

Roebuck, as Area Officer, attended the meeting at Bell's home on the last weekend in August 1964, where details concerning Kanazawa's stay in Britain for the BKF were discussed. A letter from Roebuck to Bell, dated the 2nd September, notes various motions carried at the meeting understood to be correct by Roebuck. These included, in condensed form here: 1) the annual licence fee be increased to three guineas, and that the old status of Full, Country and Associate member be discontinued (and that the increased fees would entitle each member to two free gradings a year); 2) that women and children be allowed to train at the Area Officer's discretion; 3) that a new, condensed application form be introduced – that references were no longer required, but a doctor's note, clearance form and two passport photos were still required; 4) that a beginners' training programme was agreed upon which consisted of a three month course studying the 8th kyu syllabus only.

Terry Wingrove travelled to the Rotherham *dojo* in early September 1964 and gave a course that 'all our members enjoyed … very much and are unanimous in their high regard for Mr. Wingrove' (letter from Roebuck to Bell dated the 16th September).

In a letter to Roebuck dated the 8th October, we learn that Bell charged one guinea per hour for private tuition at his home, and that this was 'the usual fee.' Roebuck obviously took up Bell's offer (letter to Bell dated the 20th October) and noted, 'I should like to say how much I enjoyed the course at your home last Monday. It was most enlightening.'

Wingrove took a six-hour course at Rotherham on the 21st November, the course fees being £13. 10. 0. A list of members who attended training showed that Roebuck, Sayles, Shaw, Hagon, Hart and Culyer were joined by J. Clark and Thompson from York. In a letter to Roebuck dated the 28th October, Bell noted the training times as follows: 9.30 a.m. – midday and 2.00 p.m. – 4.00 p.m. and 5.00 p.m. – 6.00 p.m. (which, of course, is five and a half hours). This course went well and Roebuck, in a letter to Bell dated the 24th November referred to 'the excellent tuition of Mr. Wingrove.' Wingrove returned for another weekend's training on the 20th March 1965.

In response to what is likely to have been an unsympathetic remark from Bell in a now lost letter, Roebuck, in an undated reply, though March 1965, noted: 'I am absolutely dedicated to my studies ... I insist on training for at least two hours every night.'

Bell, of course, was full-time secretary to the BKF, and this sometimes put him in an awkward position where he felt it necessary to justify his position. In response to a letter by Roebuck dated the 3rd October 1965, where his committee had discussed Bell's 'new salary, rent, etc.,' Bell responded on the 5th October, noting: 'I do fully realise the amount of work that all the Area Officers put in as unpaid officials in organising their branches, but I would also point out that they also have their full-time paid jobs as security which they had prior to taking up karate. In my case, the matter is a little different, in that as full-time secretary of the Federation, which has been brought about more by increasing demands and expansion as a national body than anything else, then I rely on drawing my weekly salary from the Federation in order to earn my living, so that I may devote all my time, every day, nearly seven days a week, to the routine affairs of the Federation. For this, I need and require the continued goodwill and close support of the Area Officers, and I have always regarded your good self as one of my most loyal and capable officers. As such, I hope you will continue to support me in the difficult task I have undertaken, and I hope we may enjoy very many future years as business colleagues.

'Both the Nottinghamshire, Portsmouth, Aberdeen and Blackpool branches have now given support to me, as well as your own branch, in the proposals put in my [lost] letter, and I thank you for your support in this matter, which has given me great personal concern for the welfare of my living and family.'

The last letter to have survived between Bell and Roebuck is a letter by Bell dated the 21st March 1966, where Bell thanks Roebuck for his report of a Wado-ryu demonstration in Sheffield. The demonstration was not considered to be that good by Roebuck and other BKF members who attended, but the audience apparently numbered about five hundred.

Page 98, line 9 – An article in an unknown newspaper by an unknown writer tells of what is believed to be Kanazawa's first visit to York. Entitled, 'Karate Star is York 'Hit,'' it reports on training in Walmgate. It confirms that Kanazawa was in York for the week and that he was to live in the UK for a year. In an interesting quote attributed to Kanazawa, the reporter notes that the discipline acquired in the practice of karate will help students become 'socially at ease.'

Two additional photographs come from this period, from an unknown source, or unknown sources. The first, hand-dated, 1965, shows training at the INL club, where three lines of students are shown in *zenkutsu-dachi* performing a left *tate-shuto* (this is almost certainly practise for *gyaku-zuki*). Trevor Collis, Neil McDonald, Tony Aydon and Stan Olsen are identifiable. There appears to be a large number of onlookers.

The other photograph shows Kanazawa performing a *yoko-tobi geri* on Gordon Thompson. In the caption, Kanazawa is credited as a 5th Dan, so the photo comes from 1965 or, it is believed, the first half of 1966.

Page 101, line 21 – David Richardson, 16, schoolboy (29.10.63).
   line 34 – Richard Johnson, 28, driver (30.10.63).
   line 37 – Christopher Douglas, 17, schoolboy (4.9.63).

Page 102, line 4 – Documents pertaining to a previously unknown Swansea Branch of the BKF appear at this time. The club only had eight members, and was organised by Warren Scott, a seventeen-year-old schoolboy who applied for BKF membership on the 13th July 1965, and accepted the position of BKF Area Officer on the 25th August 1965. From the limited correspondence, it appears that the *dojo* never really got off the ground, competing, as it was, with a Wado-ryu club in the city. Members of the Swansea *dojo* were: Alan Crimes, 19, Navy (9.1.66); Anthony Davies, 17, porter (3.4.66); Geoffrey Dudden, 18, apprentice electrician (11.4.66); Francis Jones, 21, carpenter (11.9.65); Michael Pinney, 17, apprentice electrician

(2.8.65); Lennard Powell, 18, plant operator (17.6.65); Roger Tozer, 17, schoolboy (14.12.65).

Page 108, line 30 – According to Bell, Firlej worked in an office.

    last paragraph – Other members of the London *dojo* for whom BKF application forms have been found are: John Allen, 38, warehouseman (26.12.65); Lawrence Anish, 24, textile agent (26.2.64); Suzanne Black, 25, chemist's assistant (19.2.66); William Chapman, 19, trainee turner (23.12.65); David Davis, 27, taxi driver (8.8.63); John Dougan, age and occupation unknown (-.1.65); John Duce, 22, sales represenative (28.1.64) – whilst having joined the BKF, Duce may never have trained; Gary Gardner, 19, electrical machinist (16.9.65); Martin Garland, 28, company director (6.8.64) – whilst having joined the BKF, Garland may never have trained; Leslie Gold, 324, taxi-cab driver (7.11.64); Larry Lee, 30, tailor's cutter (11.2.65); Han Ling, 18, reporter (12.3.65); Thomas Love, 35, warehouse assistant (29.8.64); Walter McCann, 18, fitter (30.12.63); Paul McMahon, 26, painter/decorator (3.1.65); Christopher Meiklejohn, 22, commercial artist (1.12.65); Leslie O'Byrne, 45, company representative (8.11.65); John Plant, 22, packer (1.12.64); Anthony Richmond, 21, camera assistant (10.3.64); Thomas Scanlon, 29, tailor's presser (19.8.63) – Scanlon was from Glasgow and was recommended to the BKF by Ainsworth. Scanlon worked as a valet at the Savoy before returning to Scotland, unemployed. Brian Shore, 30, boiler operator (7.4.64); John Skipper, 24, roofing estimator (27.7.64); Guy Taplin, 24, lifeguard (12.8.63) – whilst Taplin became a BKF member, it appears he never trained; Vaughan Toms, 18, electrician's mate (19.12.65); Martin Ward, 18, furniture salesman (10.1.62); Denis Wink, 23, merchant seaman (11.12.65).

    An Edward Tindale, aged twenty-four, and a barrister's clerk by occupation, applied for membership to the BKF on the 4th April 1963, with Neal and Bounds sponsoring him. Bell, however, was unhappy with the application, and apparently returned the forms. What is curious about Tindale, unless there has been an error, is that for his permanent address, he gave the Horseshoe Pub, Clerkenwell – the BKF London *dojo* at the time.

    Three additional membership forms were included in this 'London batch,' though it is unknown whether these individuals – Denis Hanson, 37, area manager (29.7.60); Eric Parker, 27, patent consultant (16.8.64), and Barry Redfearn, 22, building contract management trainee (7.10.64) – were members of the London *dojo*, for they lived in Lancashire, Sussex and Cornwall, respectively.

Page 109, line 8 – Wingrove was living in Japan by October 1968, and in November that year was residing at 37, Matsukaze-cho, Nishinomiya-shi, Hyogo-ken.

Page 111, line 32 – The Hyson Green Community Centre was located in St. Paul's Avenue (off Radford Road), Hyson.

Page 114, line 19 – Bell's parents moved to 180 Walton Rd, Walton-on-the-Naze, Essex, on the 1st June 1963 (letter from Bell to M. Russell, 7th May 1964).

Page 115, line 27 – There is at least one incident of Bell taking Kanazawa to see a karate demonstration. Nick Adamou recalled, as a 7th kyu, attending a display at a town hall in London given by a here un-named Japanese instructor, along with Bell, Kanazawa, and a number of other BKF students. Adamou recalled: 'Although I found it interesting, after having seen Kase, Kanazawa, Enoeda and Shirai do karate demonstrations, well, there was just no comparison … Some days/weeks after this demonstration, I remember hearing Mr. Bell talking about Mr. Kanazawa's reaction to it as he sat in the audience, and Mr. Bell said that Kanazawa's face was red with embarrassment because he thought the way ——— was performing karate looked like about purple-belt level.'

Page 120, line 12 – Lilleshall Hall was described at the time in the CCPR '1965-1966 Christmas/New Year Sports Coaching Courses,' as 'the second CCPR National Recreation Centre to be opened. Its extensive grounds are as beautiful in winter as in summer … The bedrooms accommodate from two to seven people, some having curtained cubicles, and the common rooms are large and comfortable.'
    Considerable correspondence has survived between Bell and officials at the Central Council for Physical Recreation (a forerunner of the Sports Council) surrounding the 1965 course. The first letter of enquiry in this regard was sent by Bell to a Mr. J. Barry, London and South-Eastern regional officer for the CCPR, on the 14th April 1965. Barry attended the visiting JKA instructors display at Hornsey as a VIP, and was interested, though in a letter of the 29th April, he thought that it was unlikely there would be availability that year to accommodate a BKF course on CCPR premises. Bell applied for BKF

THE BRITISH KARATE-DO FEDERATION

Incorporating
KARATE CLUB OF BRITAIN

(Directly affiliated to JAPAN KARATE ASSN. which is ONLY legally constituted
Body recognized by Japan Ministry of Education)

B.K.F. is ONLY authorized organization for BRITAIN of J.K.A., TOKYO
for development and control of KARATE-DO System of FUNAKOSHI-GICHEN

Resident National Coach/Technical Director/Chief Grader and European Delegate of J.K.A.:
Master HIROKAZU KANAZAWA (5 Dan)

National Secretary/Organizer: V. C. F. BELL, Ps.D., Ms.D.
(Shodan of J.K.A.),
91, Perryman's Farm Road,
Newbury Park, Ilford, Essex.
Val. 7705 (10 a.m.–5 p.m.)

Date ......3rd March, 1966

Your Ref. ....

Our Ref. ....

Established Branches at

ABERDEEN

BLACKPOOL

DUNDEE

LONDON

LIVERPOOL

MANCHESTER

ROTHERHAM

UPMINSTER

YORK

AYR

BATH

BRADFORD

HULL

LEEDS

LEICESTER

MANCHESTER

PORTSMOUTH

PLYMOUTH

RAINFORD

SWANSEA

CERTIFICATE OF PROFICIENCY

This is to certify that E. WHITCHER of 52 Butterfield
Road .... attended and
participated in the Senior Kyu Grade Instructor's
Summer course at the Grange Farm Centre, Chigwell,
Essex, under the instruction of Mr.H.Kanazawa. 5th
Dan of the JKA for the period September 11th - 18th,
1965 and reached the satisfactory standard in Kate,
Kumite and teaching techniques equivalent to the
Brown Belt Junior Instructor Grade status of the
Federation. No grading examination was partaken
on this course.

Signed.

V.C.F.Bell
National Secretary.

H.Kanazawa
Technical Director.

Edward Whitcher's Junior Instructor's certificate signed by Kanazawa and
Bell – 1965 (II/115). Nothing whatsoever is known about the BKF branches
in Ayr (assuming this is not Saltcoats), Hull, Leeds and Leicester (assuming
this is not the 1962/63 BKF *dojo*).

accommodation on the 13th May to run a summer course and, aware
of the late booking, was prepared to accept Bisham Abbey (near
Marlow, Buckinghamshire), Crystal Palace (Norwood, London SE19)
or Lilleshall Hall, and then applied to all three directly. Only Lilleshall
was available, and after Bell's initial enquiry to the centre on the 18th
May, he secured the course with a five guinea deposit (letter to J. Lane,
the centre's warden, dated the 25th May).

Lane's letter to Bell dated the 31st May, reveals that Ford Hall was to be used for training, which was approximately twenty-five yards in length by twenty-two yards in width, and had a maple floor. Two additional side rooms were also offered. The training accommodation was very acceptable to Bell. In a letter to Lane dated the 15th June, Bell noted that Kanazawa had chosen the following times for daily training: 6.00 a.m. – 8.00 a.m. before breakfast, 4.30 p.m. – 6.30 p.m., before dinner. The first course was intended to begin at 4.30 p.m. on Saturday, 24th August, and the last course session was on the following Saturday at 6.00 a.m. In a letter dated the 10th August, Bell wrote to Lane noting: 'I will be glad if you could arrange the best accommodation you can for our Japanese teacher, Mr. Kanazawa, and preferably, if you have a small private room near the Ford Hall where he can sleep and be on his own, for he likes privacy and rest, but if this is not possible, would you please see that he gets a corner bed in the best situation in one of your chalets.'

Lane replied on the 12th August: 'I will see to it that Mr. Kanazawa has a single room in our new block.'

A list of trainees from the Lilleshall course has survived. The names shown are: G.Aaron, C. Adamou, N. Adamou, M. Barrington, J. Boughen, R. Burgin, S. Cattle, B. Cooper, Miss D. Draper, D. Hepworth, J. Johnson, J. Johnston, P. Judge, D. Lindsay, S. Longstaff, I. MacLaren, M. O'Keefe, T. Parsons, C. Patterson, K. Roebuck, K. Sayles, P. Smith, A Stewart, J. Taylor, K. Taylor, Miss W. Varley. In a letter to Lane dated the 24th August 1965, Bell adds three additions: N. Andrew, R. Gale, R. Hannington. In this letter, Bell requests that when arranging sleeping accommodation, Lane puts members of the same *dojos* together. As the photograph of the course members shows (on page 120), Alan Smith and Andy Sherry make the numbers up to the thirty-one photographed.

Bell had written to Roebuck on the 26th August 1965, asking him, as he was the only Area Officer attending the course, to liase between Kanazawa and the authorities at Lilleshall (namely, Mr. J. Lane), and, indeed, in a letter to Lane of the same date, Bell wrote: 'Mr. Roebuck, who is the Area Officer of our Rotherham Branch, is to be put in-charge of the course.'

Bell had been contacted by a Mr. J. Bradley of the CCPR (letter dated the 4th August), asking whether he would like to book for 1966. Bell replied on the 10th, noting he would like a week at Bisham Abbey from the 7th-14th May, a week at Crystal Palace from the 23rd-30th July, and a week at Lilleshall from the 3rd-10th September. Bell continued: 'It is expected that on each course we shall obtain between thirty and fifty resident pupils, and maybe more now that these courses are planned well ahead, and karate is growing very quickly at the moment and is getting widely known and we have an extensive programme next year.' A week at Crystal Palace between the 30th July and the 6th August 1966, was all that was available and Bell took it (letter to Bradley dated the 7th September). Emlyn Jones, director of the Crystal Palace National Recreation Centre, wrote to Bell on the 3rd January 1966, noting that a training hall measuring fifty-seven feet by thirty-four feet, with a 'rather expensive Rhodesian teak floor' had been booked for the intended BKF course. Bell secured reserved places for this course from the following BKF members: G. Aaron, C. Adamou, N. Adamou, J. Johnson, P. Judge, F. Lomax, M. Peachey, A. Stewart, J. Taylor. The intended BKF Crystal Palace course never actually went ahead, nor did any of the others.

Page 121, line 15 – Nick Adamou had two further recollections of the evening of the last night of the Lilleshall course before returning home that are worthy of note, for very different reasons. The first showed how much Adamou held Kanazawa in awe, as did many others, the second, in complete contrast, reveals how another acted in the presence of the master.

Nick recalled sitting on a leather chair in a pub, next to Kanazawa, with others around a table. 'It was a great atmosphere as everyone chatted and joked amongst each other and with Kanazawa *Sensei* – just a wonderful end to a wonderful course. I remember how nervous I felt seated next to this giant of a person, who exuded so much energy or presence, and who felt like royalty. This may sound strange, but when I visited a zoo in Vienna, there was a tiger in a cage that was pacing up and down … constantly watching all of us watching him. The tiger was about five feet away and you could just feel its power, its energy, its spirit … This was the feeling I got when I was seated beside Kanazawa *Sensei* on that occasion, and I've experienced it on many other occasions with him. Anyway, *Sensei* was asked many questions about karate, Japan, fighting, and so on, and I was desperate to ask him a question. I was eighteen years old, a very shy and nervous person, and I took gulps of shandy in order to boost my confidence. Every now and again, just as I felt the inspiration to 'go for it,' and put a question to him when a gap appeared in the conversation, *Sensei* turned his head towards me as if he felt I was going to dare to speak. And, just as I was about to, and just when he looked at me, I froze and just couldn't say a word. *Sensei* turned his head to face in the other direction in such a way as to not show me that he had been expecting a question from me, and that he had seen that I had backed down at the last moment. He didn't want me to lose face, and he didn't want me to give up by feeling even worse.

'As soon as another moment arose, and I had built myself up with more shandy, and had mentally rehearsed what I was going to say, and was convinced that, 'Yes. This is it,' ... *Sensei* turned to face me ... and I just couldn't say a thing. This ... happened two more times, and each time *Sensei* turned to face me, it seemed that he knew the dilemma I was going through. Just like the times when I've paced up and down on a diving board, convincing myself that, yes, now is definitely the time when I'm going to dive in, but don't, until eventually some kind of cut-off mechanism kicks in and I just do it, I said, '*Sensei*.' As I was about to ask my question, Kanazawa said, 'Yes, Mr. Adamou,' in an explosion of joy, as if he was hoping and waiting for me to find the courage.

'*Sensei* had always spoken about 'pushing the *hara* down' ... Well, I'd always wondered whether the same thing was true in the other direction, in other words, whether one should 'feel up with the *hara*' when performing flying-kicks, for example. When I finally explained this to *Sensei*, with the sound of my heart ringing in my ears, *Sensei* was overjoyed and said, 'Yes. Good question. Yes, it's true. You must think and feel up with your *hara* for jumping kicks.' Although *Sensei* seemed to like my question, I'm sure that he was more pleased with the fact that I had defeated my own inner fear by daring to ask it. This was a very wonderful moment for me and I've always remembered it.'

But not all BKF students were so reverential. On the journey back to the dormitory at Lilleshall, Nick and Chris Adamou shared a taxi with Kanazawa, and two other BKF members. Adamou continued with the second recollection: '—— and —— [names omitted] jumped out of the taxi to get some winkles, whelks and the like from a stall and once back in the taxi they offered some to *Sensei*, Chris and I. Suddenly, —— turned his head away from *Sensei*, who was seated beside him and proceeded to stick a whelk up his nose. After a bit of pushing and manoeuvring, the whelk was finally lodged in —— nose and at that point he turned to *Sensei* and said, 'Look *Sensei*.' *Sensei* turned ... [and] —— made the movements with his fingers against the whelk as if he was picking his nose. Kanazawa *Sensei* kind of nodded his head and laughed a bit.'

line 32 – In contrast, Kanazawa always seemed to be

aware of the possibility of being attacked. Nick Adamou recalled an incident at the Lyndhurst Hall *dojo*: 'One of the women students shouted out, 'Kanazawa *Sensei*!' and he literally stopped dead in his tracks as if he was waiting for an attack.'

Page 122, line 38 – Thompson continued: 'He [Kanazawa] hated the poky little flat he had been given, he resented being chivvied around by Mr. Bell, and listed a lot of other grievances as best as he could with his limited command of English. I cannot remember all of them after nearly forty years, but by then I was becoming a bit wary and suspected him of laying things on a bit thick. We did not worship him in the manner he was becoming accustomed to. I often got the impression he was looking for a pedestal to stand on and we didn't stock them up here.'

Page 127, line 35 – The date for Bindra's sojourn was from the 13th May 1965 for 'approximately six to eight weeks' (letter to Bell dated the 8th May 1965). In a letter to Bindra dated the 27th July 1965, Bell notes that the sum owed was £5. 12. 6.

Page 133, line 14 – An interesting free-hand letter comes from Andy Sherry at this time to Bell. The letter date is unclear, but looks like 11.10.65, but whether it's the 11th October or the November 10th is speculative, for Sherry's letters at the time tended to be undated, though the former is the more likely. The letter reads: 'We have been informed by Mr. Green that you intend to enter a team to contest in the BKA tournament. The Liverpool Branch wish to very strongly object on the grounds that: 1) none of the BKF members have been taught freestyle sparring by *Sensei*, or in fact by any other master; 2) *Sensei* intends to hold the BKF tournament next year inviting all clubs. Unlike the BKA, he said he wanted to hold them this year but no one is good enough yet; 3) we think that *Sensei* will be extremely displeased, as we think it is against his wishes.'

Page 138, line 39 – In a letter to Roebuck dated the 5th October 1965, Bell writes of Rousseau, so: 'I very much regret to tell you that Mr. Rousseau has seen fit to return to South Africa last Saturday, 2nd, to enter Johannesburg University, since he could not enter London University within a year. So I regret I cannot offer him for a course, and it is a great disappointment to us all for he was well liked.'

Members of the York *dojo* taken in St. Clement's Church Hall – 1965. From left to right, back row: Gordon Thompson, Ian Gray, Ian MacLaren, John Clark, unknown, unknown, George Smith, Don Gowland. Front row: Neil MacDonald, Mary MacLaren, Stephen Cattle, Trevor Collis, Douglas Aston, Michael O'Donovan, unknown, unknown, Patrick O'Donovan. Donald Dent and Anthony Aydon are between rows.

After leaving the INL, the BKF York *dojo* moved to St. Clement's Church Hall in Moss Street. Entry was, in fact, via the other side of the building, but it was at this *dojo* that the York club expanded – so much so, infact, that a waiting list was in operation. The floor was slippery, but not to the extent of the INL *dojo*, and the club was left in peace to train. Kanazawa never visited this *dojo* under the BKF. Photo: 2002.

Page 139 – A newspaper article, of unknown origin, by an uncredited reporter, provides a few details concerning the trip to Australia made by Trevor Collis. Entitled, 'Karate Experts Off to Australia,' the short piece notes that Collis was intending to travel with two fellow York students – Ian Gray and Neil McDonald. Collis's occupation was given as an agricultural engineer. At the time of the article, Gray was a 5th kyu, and Collis and McDonald, 6th kyu. McDonald is quoted: 'We wanted to go to Japan to get black belts … but a leading Japanese master who came to York recently advised us to go to Australia first. He said we should make money teaching karate there before going to Japan. We plan to start a club in Sydney … They all expect to return to this country later to teach karate professionally.'

There is also a photograph from an unknown newspaper, but hand-dated the 4th July 1966. With the caption, *Off to Australia*, it notes that Gray and Collis are off 'tomorrow' to start instructing in karate for eighteen months. Then, 'They are going to Japan for two years to get their black belts.' Of course Collis was killed in Australia, though what became of Gray (and McDonald, if he went) is unknown.

The said photograph shows Collis in *kamae* with Gray kicking him *chudan mae-geri* as Kanazawa holds Gray's lower leg in the correct position.

Page 141, after accounts – In a document entitled, 'Commitments for London Branch,' we get the following weekly budget for Kanazawa for the period 21st November 1965 to 13th February 1966:

	£	s	d
Weekly wage	25	0	0
Weekly Income Tax	5	5	0
Weekly Insurance Stamp	1	6	9
Overtime Sunday morning, Upminster	5	0	0
Rent on flat	6	0	0
Electric and gas on flat	1	0	0
Food allowance	7	0	0
Dojo rent	10	10	0
Travel expenses *dojo* to flat		15	0
TOTAL	£61	16	9

Bell noted that the 'number of practising London members at [the] time of this notice – 45.' The cost of training was 25/- per student per

week, three months in advance. Kanazawa would teach five nights a week at the *dojo*, and on Sundays at Upminster (between 10 a.m. and 1.30 p.m.). London students were also advised that: 'Instead of payment for two <u>set</u> classes as in the past, ALL active members will now share equally in the running costs of the London *dojo* ... So from the newest novice to the highest kyu grade, without exception, all members pay the same fee, for all members receive the same benefits and the same knowledge from Mr. Kanazawa's teaching.'
    line 7 – Marczak is also recorded as 'Marcjak.'

Page 144, line 1 – Stewart Duncan was a member of the BKF when Anderson knew him, having applied for membership on the 2nd May 1963, as a twenty-seven year old clerk. After attending a course under Murakami at Middlesbrough, Duncan tried to establish a *dojo* in Aberdeen, but what became of it is unknown.

Page 145, line 22 – John Mitchell, 18, clerk (19.9.65); Henry Morrice, 17, electrician (19.11.65); Robert Noble, 19, student (22.11.64); George Rennie, 27, draughtsman (18.3.66); Ronald Robertson, 20, joiner (21.12.65); Donald Ross, 15 schoolboy (26.4.64); Eric Scott, 31, power loom tuner (18.7.63); Archibald Simm, 27 steel erector (18.3.66); William Smith, 22, scaffolder (6.2.66); Thomas Sprott, 17, storeman (16.3.65); Kenneth Stopani, 17, schoolboy (15.11.64); D. Taylor, 22, student (29.11.64); Angus Watt, 30, male nurse (15.10.65); Ronald Watt, 18, machine man (16.3.66); Alexander Williamson, 29, veterinary surgeon (27.11.65); George Wood, 16, schoolboy (12.4.64).
    line 37 – Glave, Hepworth and Sayles were Rotherham members.
    line 37 – D. Hepworth is almost certainly the P. Hepworth of an earlier grading (p. 97). The initial 'D' is correct.

Page 147, line 3 – Members of the BKF Manchester *dojo* for whom membership forms have survived are: Barrie Abbott, 23, structural engineer (1.11.64); Margaret Abbott, 22, aerodynamicist (5.3.65); Walter Ainscough, 50, director (8.4.64) – at the time of his application, Ainscough was a black belt from the Robinson Brothers in judo/ju-jitsu; N. Andrew, 18, labourer (4.5.65); Michael Bagnall, 22, law student (18.5.66); Carol Banks, 23, housewife (4.3.65); Thomas Banks, 24, director (11.1.65); Edward Bench, 19, civil servant (26.9.64) – Bench was branch officer; Anthony Broadhurst, 20, sheet metal worker (29.12.65); Brian Broadwith, 18, student (25.1.66); Jack Dewhirst, 16, schoolboy (24.1.66); Michael Donnan, 19, student (20.1.66); Patrick Early, 30, driver (8.7.65); Christopher Gogarty, 17, apprentice printer (14.2.64); Christopher Gordon, 18, student (19.5.66); David Grundy, 24, building contractor (15.9.64); Peter Hales, 31, representative (1.12.65); Brian Hanrahan, 28, centre lathe turner (9.2.66); Terence Heaton, 37, office manager (20.11.64); Ian Hornby, 17, trainee draughtsman (8.5.65); Paul Hudson, 17, apprentice engineer (25.1.66); David Hughes, 19, insurance clerk (26.10.65); Albert Jones, 31, sales representative (23.12.65); Robert Jones, 26, bricklayer (10.1.66); Robert Jones, 16, schoolboy (12.4.65); Thomas Kilpatrick, 23, driver (-.-.66); John Manchester, 31, paper mill turbine driver (20.9.65); Peter Maude, 23, journalist (28.1.66); Gordon McKenna, rubber spreader (20.1.66); Michael McNamara, 16, apprentice electrical engineer (20.1.66); William Oakley, 24, painter/decorator (6.1.66); Stephen Patterson, 23, printer (31.1.66); James Pearson, 34, ship's rigger (2.1.66); Ronald Pilkington, 32, animal beautician (27.12.65); Keith Robinson, 17, clerical assistant (26.4.65); Ronald Roe, 27, painter/decorator (6.1.66); Ian Rowley, 19, student (26.1.66); Eric Royle, 17, hand engraver of precious metals (26.1.66); Robert Senior, 20, clerk (28.9.65); Michael Toze, 22, quality controller (19.1.66); Malcolm Whitney, 29, architect (18.1.66); Arthur Wright, 20, travelling showman (5.2.66); William Wright, 19, draughtsman (26.10.64) – Wright acted as *dojo* secretary.

     line 7 – 'Andred' should read 'Aldred' (and on page 199)

     line 8 – 'Hufton' should read 'Hupton' (and on page 201)

     line 10 – 'M. Shoulder' should read 'M. Shovler' (and on page 204).

     line 10 – 'J. Summers' is likely to be 'D. Summers' (and on page 204).

Page 149, line 12 – Many students, certainly Kanazawa's closest London students, have stories to tell concerning the master. Nick Adamou recalled: 'I remember on many occasions, through different grades … to brown belt, travelling on the underground with Kanazawa *Sensei* and sitting opposite him. He would sometimes just suddenly look straight at me, stare right through me, like a glare. I used to be so embarrassed and had no idea what to do. Should I stare back? Should I turn away? What on earth was going on? Why was he doing this? Then, seconds later, he'd do a kind of biting of his lip, which made him look fed up, agitated, angry, and he'd simply turn away. Seconds after that, he would start to talk about something nice or interesting. I always got the feeling that whilst in the presence of this very special human being, you were going to go through many experiences in the name of learning.'

line 17 – The 'gods' were continuously being scrutinised, and once error was detected, interesting reactions ensued. Nick Adamou cites an example of this, not long after his first grading under Kanazawa, regarding an incident that took place on the Northern Underground Line, when he accompanied the master, alone. Nick realised, just as the train doors were closing, that they should have got off the train. Kanazawa, 'with the doors about eighteen inches apart … put his arms through the gap and started doing *kakiwake-uke*. He was wearing his usual grey trousers, Hush Puppy shoes, white shirt and tie, and blue raincoat. As he struggled with the mechanical workings of the doors, in order to re-open them, he went through three different stance changes, and I noticed that his shoulders came up as he performed the wedge-block. I felt ashamed of myself for noticing his shoulders being raised, for every time we trained in *Heian Yondan*, in which this block is performed, *Sensei* always told us to keep them down.'

It is interesting to get a reaction from individuals who were not so enchanted with the Japanese, and once again Nick Adamou provides us with an example. Kanazawa, and some of his closest London disciples, went to the Adamou house in Wood Green for a meal. Nick recalled: 'Kanazawa *Sensei* sat in a chair most of the time talking about various things. As he did so, he would quite often do some twisting moves with his arms – *ude-uke, uchi-uke, shuto-uke,* and so on – and some leg movements, twisting inward and outward as in *kiba-dachi* and *shiko-dachi*. My father, who is a very confident, natural, down to earth type of person, must have been watching all these movements – the sort of movements that we had got used to, and which, in fact, we did all over the place.

'After Kanazawa *Sensei* left, Chris and I asked our father for his impressions of our instructor. My father said, 'Okay. But, he's a very nervous man.' We couldn't believe that our father could say this and we asked why. He replied, 'He's not relaxed and keeps moving his hands and feet like a very nervous man.' Chris and I instantly rallied to Kanazawa *Sensei's* defence, explaining that he was so involved with his karate technique, always thinking about it, that it was part of his body and being … He's testing them out all the time for his own perfection [we argued]. My father would have none of it, and told us that we were hypnotized with this 'karate stuff.'"

Page 155, last line – On page 5 of the October 1966 edition of *Karate News*, Sherry and Chialton's grading date is given as the 6th February 1966.

Page 156, line 12 – We now know that Sherry and Chialton's *Shodan* grades were definitely in February 1966. In an 'Official Notice From the Secretary's Office' Bell recorded: 'We are pleased to announce that promotions to the Dan grades have been granted in February to Mr. J. Neal, 1st Dan, of London (see below [on page 156]), Mr. J. Green, 1st Dan of Blackpool, Mr. J. Chialton, 1st Dan, and Mr. A. Sherry, 1st Dan, of Liverpool.' In the second of only two known text references to BKF/JKA black-belts at this time, Bell wrote to a Mr. Humphreys of the CCPR (who had written to Bell with regard to an enquiry he had received from a Mr. Griffiths about karate in Rhyl), noting that: 'I would suggest that Mr. Griffiths contacts our two local branches, where we have two qualified black-belts, who, I am sure, would agree to a combined display in Rhyl. Please contact Mr. A. Sherry, 1st Dan, 2b Canterbury Way, Liverpool 6, of the Liverpool karate club, and Mr. J. Green, 1st Dan, Green Star Garage, 363a Lytham Road, Blackpool, of the Blackpool karate club, both of whom are our area representatives.'

Page 158, line 8 – Lance Applegate, 19, accounts clerk (22.12.65). Colin Hamiliton, 19, chef (29.12.65). Gerald Levy, 34, sales representative (6.12.65). David Parry, 23, clerk (6.12.65). Donald Sinclair, 23, garage attendent (9.1.66).

      line 9 – Robert Zamenhof, 19, student (25.12.65). Louis Harper, 32, warehouseman (7.1.66).

      line 10 – Bayliss was a haulier. Jeffrey Brooks, 33, administrator (25.11.65). According to Bell, Singh was a student.

Page 160, line 8 – Eleven new, single-page Application for Membership/Licence forms have been discovered in a batch, all from 1966. Ten of these forms are headed, 'Karate-Do Association (affiliated to BKF and JKA),' and are in a much abbreviated format. The remaining one, Baird's, was made direct to the BKF in a similar abbreviated format to that shown in Vol. I, pages 252-253, though different from the other ten. There is anecdotal information to suggest that Baird was aligned to the Chiswick *dojo*. Using the usual format of name, age at the time of application, occupation, and date of application (in brackets), the additional applications forms are: Harry

Baird, age unknown, actor (20.3.66); Alan Boast, 25, film technician (2.2.66); Robert Cook, age unknown, student (12.2.66); Gerry Crampton, age unknown, stunt director (8.3.66); Frank Elliott, 25, film technician (2.2.66); John Gilbert, 25, films (1.3.66); John Morris, 30, actor (2.2.66); Raymond Stamford, age unknown, fireman (15.1.66); Richard Strange, 23, plasterer (1.2.66); Stanley Twist, 28, commercial artist (8.2.66); Geoffrey Williams, 19, assistant manager (2.2.66).

line 15 – In certain *dojos* at this time, children were now actively beginning encouraged to take karate up. In an unknown newspaper, of unknown date (though almost certainly 1965), by an unknown reporter, *Boys Learn the 007 Bond Way,* provides the uninformed reader with a description of karate. Vernon Bell is quoted so: 'This system cannot be mis-used in a street fight. It is a sport devised to attain physical fitness and mental and physical co-ordination.' The article, which comes from a local paper, is accompanied by a picture of Kanazawa instructing at the British Legion Hall, Upminster.

In another article in an unknown paper, of unknown date, by an unknown author, entitled, 'No Peril in TV Karate,' it is explained that, 'the British Medical Association was called in by the National Association of Headteachers, who feared the possibility of a karate 'telly menace.'' The article reports that the BMA gave the problem to its committee of medical science, education and research, who dealt with the matter. Doctor H. Evans Robson, principal lecturer in anatomy and physiology at Loughborough Training College, is quoted as saying, 'it is doubtful whether karate has been copied by children from TV programmes. It is not only a highly developed skill, but also demands muscular development which children would hardly have attained.' The piece concludes: 'The remarkable thing is that anyone imagines that even children take TV programmes seriously.'

Nick Adamou recalled two incidences that are believed related to the Chiswick *dojo*. Whilst karate training was growing in popularity, it would be erroneous to think that every lesson given by a Japanese master was well attended. Adamou recalled: 'The session that evening at the Chiswick *dojo*, I think, was taken by Enoeda *Sensei* and there were only four people present ... [after the lesson Adamou was disgusted that so few students had trained]. As Enoeda *Sensei* had finished getting changed, he walked up to us and looked at me.

'Mr. Adamou, what is the matter?' he asked. '*Sensei,* it is bad that there were only four students here to train under you,' I replied.

Enoeda said, 'It doesn't matter if there are a hundred students or just one. I am happy to teach karate. Must have karate spirit all the time!'

The second recollection is a humorous one. Adamou continued: 'I was … sitting on a train with my brother and Enoeda *Sensei*. We were returning to London from Barnes after having been to the Chiswick *dojo*. A situation arose in which someone rushed passed us and pushed either Chris, or myself, I can't remember, as we got out of the train. Enoeda *Sensei*, Chris and I sat back in a black taxi, and my brother and I started to discuss the pros and cons of performing a *gyaku-zuki* to the man who pushed by. Suddenly, Enoeda *Sensei* bellowed, 'No!' and my brother and I looked at each other and thought, 'Oh my God! We shouldn't have said that.' However, Enoeda *Sensei* continued: 'No *gyaku-zuki* – must use *mae-geri*!' and we all laughed heartily.'

Page 162, line 10 – In a letter to Gardner dated the 24th February 1966, we learn that Kanazawa's address was 59c, Compayne Gardens, Hampstead, London NW5. This address is later confirmed in a letter to Bode.

Page 163, line 8 – As Bindra noted, it was indeed rare for a woman to practise karate at this time, but the media were beginning to take an interest and women were starting to practise. Tricia Manners, in the last of three articles on women's defence, entitled, 'Chop Him Down to Size,' which appeared on page 18 of the *Romford Recorder* on Thursday 17th March 1966, describes karate training at the Ben David Judo Club. Interested readers were advised to contact L. Palmer, the secretary to the British Karate Association, at 77 Cambridge Road, Wimbledon. Two photographs accompany the piece – one shows Manners kicking *mae-geri*, but clearly indicates she doesn't know karate, and the other shows her thrusting her thumbs to an opponent's neck.

In an unknown newspaper by an unknown writer, a short article entitled, 'Karate Masters Show York How,' we see a photo of Mary MacLaren performing a left *jodan empi* on Master Enoeda, with Master Kanazawa at her other side. The picture was taken on the evening of the York club's dinner at the Apollo Room, and all three are so attired. The article contains an historically interesting, if unclear quote: 'It cost the clubs £2000,' said York club member Ian MacLaren, 'but these men earn big money in their own country.' In actual fact, karate teaching for the JKA instructors teaching in Japan before and at this time was more akin to a vocation, for instructors, the author understands, and this was particularly true of the mid to late 1950s, were very poorly paid. Perhaps the quote refers to the BKF clubs, but if it refers to the York *dojo*(s) then it is almost certain that £2000 is an incorrect figure, and the £70 mentioned later (page 190) is more realistic.

Similarly, women's use of self-defence was featured in an unknown Yorkshire newspaper by an unknown reporter of unknown date (though almost certainly 1966), with nurses training in the recreation hall of the City Hospital, York, under members of the York *dojo*. Entitled, 'Lest They be Molested ...' Three photographs are shown of two nurses performing counter-attacks – a *teisho-uchi* on Walter Knowles, a throw on Patrick O'Donovan, and a *jodan-empi* on Neil McDonald.

Page 164, line 10 – The books on Zen had yellow covers.

line 17 – Nick Adamou provides us with an account of what he thought might be considered telepathy. Adamou recalled: 'We were about to turn right into the Finchley Road, and there was a blind man at the traffic lights and he wasn't sure what to do – cross or wait, as there was no one there to help him. The car I was in was crowded ... and I was squashed up against Kanazawa *Sensei's* leg ... As uncomfortable as this was, I could feel all these strange body moves and hear all the things that Kanazawa *Sensei* was quietly saying as he watched the blind man. He was saying things to ... encourage him [to walk across], but not out loud, and the blind man seemed to be straining his head in Kanazawa *Sensei's* direction and crossed when I heard *Sensei* quietly saying, 'Yes. Go Now.' Afterwards, *Sensei* remarked on telepathy and noted that if we lose one of our senses, we can use telepathy. He said that if we train sincerely in Karate-Do, we can develop this.

Page 166, line 20 – 'Amarr' should read 'A. Marr' (and corrected in the Index).

Page 167, line 5 – In a letter to Humphreys dated the 4th March, 1966, Bell noted that the BKF were negotiating to establish karate branches at the 'universities at Aberdeen, Hull, Leeds and Liverpool, at this time.' Bell continued: 'It is the ambition and plan of our Japanese Karate Association and its representatives in England ... to establish a British Universities Karate Association, affiliated to our own BKF, working through it and with it. We also hope, through our own Federation, to establish authentic Karate-do courses and classes in all leading cities and evening institutes and technical colleges, employing our own Japanese trained and qualified instructors.'

line 40 – Kanazawa caught the 7.30 a.m. train from Aberdeen, arriving at Newcastle at 1.12 p.m. – the ticket costing £5. 1. 1d.

Page 168, line 1 – Training at the Sunderland *dojo* was on the Saturday afternoon, with morning and afternoon sessions on the Sunday, 10th April. Kanazawa then caught the 7.51 a.m. train to London, arriving at 12.40 p.m. – the ticket costing £5. 5. 0d. He then travelled to Poole on the 1.30 p.m. arriving at 4.45 p.m. at a ticket cost of £4. 13. 0d.

line 3 – The *dojo* was based at 197, High Street.

line 4 – Alan and Harry Marr were both black belt 2nd Dan *judoka* at this time.

line 7 – 'Hansom' may read 'Hanson,' (though the initials given are different).

line 8 – 'Dun' should read 'Dunne' (and on page 200).

line 11 – Sunderland BKF members for whom details have survived, are: Brian Akenhead, 34, service engineer (9.4.66); Jeffrey Barwick, 23, hairdresser (10.4.66); Robert Bewley, 26, melter (10.4.66); John Budd, 42, engineer (—.—.66); Robert Colman, apprentice draughtsman 18, (15.5.66); Peter Davidson, 23, chemist (10.4.66); Robert Dunn, 31, plumber (10.4.66); James Eblett, 26, painter (9.4.66); Robert Fambely, 34, teacher (10.4.66); Richard Hanson, 23, plumber (9.4.66); Richard Holborg, 18, joiner (10.4.66); John Holdsworth, 18, junior surveyor (10.4.66); Graeme Hollyhead, age unknown, counterman (10.4.66); Hugh Kelly, 18, clerk (9.4.66); Thomas McDonald, 19, driver (10.4.66); Lance Noble, 17, security engineer (10.4.66); Bruce Parkin, 19, apprentice fitter/mechanic (—.—.66); Derek Richardson, 19, painter (—.—.66); Terence Robson, 18, clerk (10.4.66); Derreck Siddell, 23, metallurgist (16.5.66); Ken Smith, 42, electric welder (9.4.66); Dennis Stobbart, 27, baths attendant (10.4.66); Douglas Towers, 19, student (10.4.66); David Woodward, 17, clerk (10.4.66).

Application forms reveal that Towers and Woodward had graded to 8th kyu under Wado-ryu's Master Suzuki in 1965, Stobbart to 7th kyu.

It will be noticed that the majority of application forms were signed on the 9th or 10th April 1966. Bell returned the licences collectively, bar two, on the 28th June 1966, in reply to a letter from Ken Smith

Malcolm Gill – BKF Bradford *dojo,* 1963 (II/168)

dated the 24th June.

Correspondence, in the form of sixteen letters, has been found between Bell and the Sunderland *dojo*, some of which will be discussed here. The first, from Alan Marr to Bell, is dated the 18th March 1966, 'regarding the possibility of joining your association.' Marr continued: 'May I explain this club is the largest in the north of England with over two hundred practising karate members …' [though only twenty-four appear to have joined the BKF]. Marr continued that they had been let down twice by a Japanese karate instructor when courses had to be cancelled, and they'd had enough. Bell replied on the 24th March, inviting the club to join the BKF, and arranged for Kanazawa to visit the *dojo* on Saturday, 9th April, conducting a course from 3.00 p.m. to 5.00 p.m. and on the following day from 11.00 a.m. to 1.00 p.m. and 3.00 p.m. to 5.00 p.m. at £2. 10. 0. per hour. In addition to this, the club were obliged to pay Kanazawa's first-class train fare 'which is always his necessity' from Aberdeen to Newcastle, and from Newcastle to London, and a meal allowance for both journeys. As the club had been Wado-ryu, Bell noted that he had explained the situation to Kanazawa, who had decided to make a decision about grading after the course. Each member was required to pay three-quarters of the BKF annual licence fee, which was £2. 2. 0. in 1966. An annual club affiliation fee of £2. 2. 0. was also payable. Bell also offered Marr the position of BKF Area Officer, Sunderland

District 'to manage our affairs within your club and the surrounding area.' Bell recalled that, 'The Marr brothers had an excellent reputation in the judo world. They were BJA, which is a good association, and they were legitimate. I never met them, but if I hadn't known of them, I wouldn't have taken the Sunderland club on board.'

Marr replied on the 30th March, accepting the course details and paying the required monies. It was proposed that Kanazawa would stay with Marr at his home at 83, Redhouse Road, Heburn-on-Tyne, County Durham. Marr was concerned that his members had not graded for a year, and wanted a grading. He also requested another one hundred licence forms, and noted that training times were Monday, Wednesday and Thursday, 7.30 p.m. to 9.30 p.m. and Sunday, 11.30 a.m. to 1.30 p.m. Marr also wondered whether Kanazawa would 'have any objection to appear on television or in a large Sunderland night club.'

Bell replied to Marr on the 4th April, noting receipt of monies and providing further information about the intended course and the BKF. He had changed the times of the Sunday training from 10.00 a.m. to midday, and 2.00 p.m. to 4.00 p.m., these being Kanazawa's 'normal hours,' and Kanazawa was agreeable to a grading that evening at a fee of £2. 10. 0. per hour. If there was to be a television or large demonstration to promote the club, then it was expected that Kanazawa would be paid a fee, as was customary.

On the 14th April, Marr wrote to Bell recounting that, 'our weekend's course went very well. Thirty members attended, out of which twenty-two took a grading.' Kanazawa was paid ten shillings per person who graded, and in a letter to Marr on the 20th April, Bell noted that, 'All grading fees go to the JKA.' Apparently Kanazawa performed two demonstrations, and Bell wondered how much Kanazawa had been paid for them.

On the 3rd May, Marr wrote to Bell asking that future correspondence be sent to Ken Smith, 'who is a most able and conscious [should read, 'conscientious'] chap.' Marr also asked for 'a complete syllabus from 9th kyu to 1st kyu, as at the moment we are in the dark.' In this letter, Marr asks whether Kanazawa would be available for another course. Bell replied to this letter on the 4th May and enclosed the JKA syllabus.

Ken Smith wrote to Bell on the 6th May, accepting the office of Area Officer for the BKF, and requested that if Kanazawa was returning to Japan, then a visit from Enoeda, at Bell's suggestion, would be welcome.

A problem arose over the grading forms that needn't be gone into here, other than to say that, initially at least, it was not Bell's fault, in that Kanazawa appears to have inappropriately given them to a London student who took his time sending them to Smith. In a letter to Bell dated the 26th May, Smith wrote that, 'This [the delay in receiving the forms] is causing great upset amongst our members who are rapidly losing interest.' Problems with the forms continued when Smith, having at last received them, sent them back to Bell (on the 4th June) for the gradings to be marked up in licences paid for, but not yet received. Unfortunately, this fiasco led to a final letter from Marr and the Sunderland *dojo* on the 11th July 1966, where he threatened Bell with legal action.

The author understands that Ken Smith went on to become the first KUGB black-belt in the North-East in 1969, and later graded to 2nd Dan. John Holdsworth was the second to receive a black belt and now holds a KUGB 5th Dan. Richardson was also one of the first to reach a KUGB 1st Dan in the North-East. Bewley and Barwick became 2nd and 4th Dans of the KUGB, respectively.

line 15 – Documents pertaining to the Poole branch have now been unearthed. It was a very small club, and only three membership forms have been found, so: Dennis Bailey, 28, car sprayer, (16.2.66); Frederick Stephens, 33, plumber, (7.2.66); David Whittaker, 27, heating engineer (30.12.65), who acted as secretary-cum-treasurer. All three were members of the Kuruma Judo Club, in Poole. Whittaker wrote to Bell on the occasion of his application noting that he was, 'still trying hard to find a suitable hall in order to form a karate section in this area.' Practice at the club was three times a week. In a letter to Bell dated 3rd March 1966, a fourth member (B. Lucas) is referred to when the Poole members visited the Portsmouth *dojo* at the time of a visit by Kanazawa. Stephens appears to have left in April and fellow members were 'extremely annoyed with him, and will tell him so when we see him' (letter from Whittaker to Bell, dated 30th April). A hall was still not forthcoming, so where the members trained is unknown, though in a letter to Bell of the 1st April, Whittaker notes 'that our *dojo* is very small and just big enough for the four of us.' They were certainly very keen though, and were prepared to invite Kanazawa, 'no matter how hard it hits our pocket.' In a letter of the 16th March, Bell had written that Kanazawa was prepared to visit the club when he was free despite the small number, and continued: 'Consequently, if you can agree to the usual terms, being first-class return rail fare, the 10/- each way meal allowance, as well as his accommodation and food during his stay, plus payment of his

David Whittaker – BKF Poole *dojo*, 1965

fee £5 for two hours, or more if you wish at the same fee, all payable in advance, then I am prepared to arrange a course for you under him.' Provisional dates of the Sunday 10th and Monday 11th April were suggested, but Kanazawa's itinerary changed slightly. In his letter of the 1st April, Whittaker was worried. He and his three friends wanted the 'undivided attention' of Kanazawa. 'However, I have received a request from Mr. Hurlock of Weymouth to attend the course with his friends. Naturally, he is most welcome, but I am wondering if other *dojos* in the area will request the chance to attend when they learn about the course. If they do, and we would not wish to refuse them, then the course might easily turn out the opposite of what we had hoped for. There is nothing like enough room, and Mr. Kanazawa would spend a lot of time amongst the various grades robbing us of the intense personal tuition we are seeking. That probably sounds selfish, but I'm sure you will understand our dilemma.' Bell replied to Whittaker on the 4th April in a friendly letter, noting that it was, essentially, a private course, that selfishness did not enter the equation, and Whittaker could invite whom he wanted. Bell also noted the Poole *dojo* was 'a small hall.' Apparently, Hurlock, who had trained at the London *dojo* and graded under Kanazawa before moving to Weymouth, had been told of the course, as had Moffatt (see shortly), by Bell. Hurlock, who was described by Bell as 'a very reliable man, and a very decent chap,' was thinking of trying to establish a BKF branch in Weymouth.

Kanazawa appears to have visited the club on the Easter Monday, and this may have extended to the Tuesday (though a letter from Whittaker to Bell dated the 26th March would have discouraged this), but the instructional time, unless arrangements changed, was of four hours duration (letter from Whittaker, dated 21st March 1966 {in which Lucas is again mentioned}). The course 'turned out to be everything we had hoped for – Mr. Kanazawa really made us work hard and we learned a great deal' (letter from Whittaker to Bell, dated 17th April {and another of the 5th May}, which confirms a grading took place for three members {the grading fee being ten shillings}). Exactly a month after the first course/grading, Whittaker wrote to Bell asking if Enoeda could come to Poole in June, but as this is the last of the correspondence, the outcome is unknown. What happened to Whittaker and Bailey is also a mystery, but Lucas joined the Portsmouth *dojo* (see shortly).

Two interesting asides are to be found in the Bell/Whittaker correspondence. Firstly, Bell, in a letter of the 4th April, noted: 'Regarding the references, I return these, since the procedure of providing references has been discontinued now by the BKF.' Secondly, Whittaker, in his letter of the 30th April, enquired about whether a BKF badge exists. Bell's reply of the 4th May noted: 'I regret the BKF has no official badge as yet, for there has been no demand whatsoever from members to warrant it being produced on a national scale. However, any branch can design its own badge solely for use within its own activities.'

line 16 – A second Stoke *dojo* was run by Leonard Moss, a forty-seven year old driver, who applied for BKF membership on the 12th April 1966. Moss, a judo *Nidan*, was the senior instructor at the Stoke-on-Trent School of Judo, which was affiliated to both the AJA and BJC, and he acted as BKF Area Officer. Moss's first contact with the BKF comes from an undated letter to Bell requesting details of the Federation, and Bell replied in a letter of the 3rd March 1966, regretting the long delay in replying, but notifying Moss that he might join. Membership forms for this *dojo* have survived for: Geoffrey Alcock, 17, clerk (12.4.66); Alistair Bailey, 24, silk worker (26.4.66); Michael Bowen, 21, publicity designer (26.4.66); Harold Buckley, 41, director (7.4.66); George Burton, 20, sheet metal worker (26.4.66); Landon Davies, 29, licencee (12.4.66); Anthony Devane, 38, director (6.10.66); Ivan Hancock, 28, hairdresser (12.4.66); John Last, 18, schoolboy (12.7.66); Arthur Lawton, 26, civil servant (26.4.66); Eric Limer, 38, sheet metal worker (7.4.66); John Manley, 18, schoolboy

(26.4.66); Bernard Meakin, 27, foreman (12.4.66); Geoffrey Mountford, 15, schoolboy (12.4.66); Stuart Mountford, 17, schoolboy (12.4.66); Brian Peach, 25, turner (9.4.66); Alfred Pointon, 24, engineer (12.4.66); Henry Rafferty, 40, director (12.4.66); Joseph Rafferty, 36, engineer (12.4.66); Kenneth Rafferty, 35, foreman (12.4.66); Samuel Rafferty, 42, director (12.4.66); Joan Shaw, 29, housewife (12.4.66). Also, from correspondence we find John Clayton, 26, meter tester; Ronald Taylor, 26, fitter; Alan Tinsley, 18 year old electrician. An L. Lockett wrote to Bell acknowledging his grading card and licence on the 7th June 1966, so he was presumably a member too.

A membership form for a William Meakin, 19, mechanic (28.10.64), from Stoke, was found in a batch of membership forms from the London *dojo*. It is unknown whether Meakin was a London member, though it seems unlikely. It may be co-incidence that a Bernard Meakin is listed in Stoke in 1966. Of course, W. Meakin's membership pre-dates the second Stoke *dojo* by more than a year, and in analyses [see Appendices] he is classified as being of unknown *dojo* affiliation.

In a letter of the 6th April 1966, Bell recommended that Moss arrange a well-publicised week-end karate course for his members with a London instructor. In a later letter (dated the 23rd April), Bell notes that he has acquired a clerical assistant, which indicates his increasing workload.

There was trouble with the non-appearance of licences once more, which were, according to Bell, being printed. The non-arrival of these, and an impressive demonstration by Martin Stott in the 'local hall where about four hundred people went to watch' (letter to Bell from Moss dated 15th May 1966) put an additional strain on relations, but this appeared resolved by the 16th June (letter from Limer {who was now club secretary} to Bell of that date), but Moss wrote again on the subject on 10th July, still dissatisfied.

The correspondence between Bell and various members of the Stoke *dojo* is interesting, because it post-dates the club exodus from the BKF that resulted in the formation of the KUGB. Samuel Rafferty wrote to Bell on the 4th August noting that Bell would be visiting the club on the 4th September. An undated letter from Moss confirmed the date and gave the *dojo* address as being in Pinnox Street, Tunstall, Stoke-on-Trent. Bell had to re-schedule for the 2nd October, owing to a grading at his own *dojo*, and noted that Ron Mills, 1st Dan, would take the course. In a letter to Warren Scott of the Swansea *dojo*, dated the 9th September 1966, Bell wrote that Mills had trained with Master C. Tani, 8th Dan, in South Africa, and had graded to *Shodan* under him in April 1965.

Mills journeyed up from London by train (at a cost of £4 5s 6d) and stayed at the George Hotel, Burslem. In a letter to S. Rafferty dated the 9th September, Bell proposed that training be held between 2.30 p.m. and 4.30 p.m. and then 6.00 p.m. and 8.00 p.m. on the Saturday, and between 10.00 a.m. and Midday and 2.30 p.m. and 4.30 p.m. on the Sunday. Bell had intended procuring a Japanese instructor, and in this letter the intention is re-affirmed, for Bell noted that, 'We hope to have our own high grade Japanese from Japan by the end of this year, who will be here on an indefinite time basis.' The course was a great success, and Moss wrote to Bell on the 19th October that 'all were very pleased, and we are going to contact you regarding a visit of Mr. Mills again, as I think we got on very well together.'

Mills reported back to Bell and this gave rise to a four-and-a-half page letter, dated the 5th October, from Bell to Moss, noting the BKF procedure for engaging instructors. In this letter, Bell noted that Mills had a list of members who trained on the course, and that Messrs. Baskervilles, Bettany, Edge, Hayes, Kent, Lightfoot, Machin and Woods, had trained despite not being BKF members. Bell sent a chaser to this letter pursuing the non-licence members on the 11th October. As a postscript, Bell wrote: 'I should also like a firm reply ... relating to the visit of Mr. Tani to England, and whether your club is willing to give positive support and arrange a visit to your club.' In a letter to Bell of the 27th October, Moss explained that he was pursuing these non-licence members. In the last letter to have survived between Bell and members of the Stoke club, Bell wrote: 'I am very sorry to hear you are at a [financial] loss on Mr. Mills' course, and I understand this, for I have organised many courses myself in the past few years, many of which have left a serious debit, sometimes which I have had to pay myself.'

Page 170, line 33 – '1964' should read, 'January 1965.'

Page 175, line 38 – Files on both the Portsmouth and Plymouth *dojos* have been unearthed. The Portsmouth *dojo*, which was formed first, was established and run by Robert Moffatt, a professional footballer for Portsmouth Football Club, who applied to join the BKF on 29th August 1964, aged eighteen. Moffatt's other interests at the time of application were sketching and playing the guitar. Considerable

Robert Moffatt – BKF Portsmouth *dojo*, 1964

correspondence exists between Moffatt and Bell, and the latter remembered the former as a 'very nice fellow.' The club *dojo* was sited at the Community Centre, Southsea. Club members for whom membership application forms survive, presented in the usual format, are: Francis Amoroso, 20, able-bodied seaman, Royal Navy (17.5.66); Peter Anderson, 31, shopkeeper (8.2.66); Ian Ayland, 18, apprentice joiner (5.12.65); Peter Bisset, 26, sales representative (12.2.66); Ray Burley, 35, prison officer (8.6.66); Ronald Cook, 33, Royal Navy (4.11.65); Peter Cooper, 20, joiner (24.4.66); Roy Cull, 24, police constable (11.2.66); David Gentles, 19, labourer (—.9.65); Reginald Goldsmith, 43, maintenance supervisor (3.5.65); Michael Goodall, 19, fitter and turner (19.2.66); John Hatton, 24, labourer (19.7.65); Michael Hazel, 20, labourer (27.7.65); Robin Ingram, 19, apprentice fitter and joiner (28.8.65); Robert Kendall, 30, printer (21.3.66); Brian Lucas, 22, hairdresser (23.2.66); Ronald Miles, 22, electronic wireman (10.2.66); Derek Mills, 23, lithographer (17.1.66); Daniel O'Hanlon, 35, council workman (11.4.66); David Oliver, 26, assistant building surveyor (18.4.66); Norman Oswald, 31, Royal Navy (8.5.66); Dennio Penfold, 34, electrical fitter (6.2.66); John Pitt, 21, draughtsman (8.2.66); Peter Rippon, 33, electronic inspector (9.2.66); John Rockell, 27, driver (28.10.65); Michael Saurin, 19, commercial bodybuilder (15.3.66); Roger Stephens, 22, labourer (8.2.66); Brian Twine, 34, building worker (8.6.65); Amran Vuai, 33, press operator (18.4.66).

Cook is interesting, in that on his application form he noted that he was a *Shodan* in karate. Bell naturally followed this up and wrote to Cook, receiving an undated reply. Cook wrote: 'I started karate training in HMAS Penguin at a club run by servicemen from service personnel. The instructor was [Colonel] J.C. Laughlin, 4th Dan, Commanding Officer Australian Commando Brigade. The other instructor was H. Brady (Capt), Australian commandos. The club was a sub-branch of the Central School of Self Defence, in Yokohama, Japan. The karate taught was judo/karate used as self-defence. The grades were: 4th kyu (yellow), 3rd kyu (orange), 2nd kyu (brown – light), 1st kyu (brown – dark), *Shodan* (black). These grades are not the same as yours, nor is the karate style.'

In two letters to Moffatt, Bell notes previously unknown BKF members. In the first, dated the 27th August 1964, a Mr. T. J. Warner of London, whose employment was in the regular army, is mentioned as being an ungraded BKF London branch member. In the second, of the 3rd June 1965, John Dunne of Twerton, Bath, is introduced. There was a 'Dunne' at the London *dojo*, but his initial is unknown.

The Plymouth *dojo* was established and run by Richard Kiernan, a twenty-one year old work-study engineer from Kingsand, near Plymouth. Kiernan's other interests at the time of his application to the BKF, on the 2nd January 1966, were judo, photography and weight training. Kiernan had initial problems starting a *dojo* after four friends dropped-out (letter to Bell dated the 13th February 1966), and was down to just himself and a Mr. K. Tunnell. Bell, in a letter dated the 18th February 1966, was supportive of Kiernan's attempts, deep in the West country as he was, noting that it was better to 'lose this type' of uncommitted individual from the beginning, and explained that what he was experiencing in trying to start a BKF branch was typical, relating that, 'The Portsmouth Branch itself had the same trouble last year and has found it a struggle for the last nine months to get established, but suddenly it had an influx of members after several training courses and is now forging ahead.' Bell, suggested perseverance, and recommended Kiernan advertise, and concluded, 'I have no doubt that this set-back is disappointing to you, but it is bound to happen at some time and has occurred in all branches, but I rely on your capabilities as a genuine karate enthusiast not to be daunted by this temporary upset.'

Kiernan took Bell's advice and placed an advert in the local press. In his letter to Bell, dated the 1st March, Kiernan noted: 'The first night I received an overwhelming amount of interested parties,' but

Richard Kiernan – BKF Plymouth *dojo*, 1966

went on to explain that there was a club in Plymouth under the auspices of Master Harada, and he didn't know how best to deal with these people. Bell's reply of the 3rd March is interesting, for he gives more information on his feelings towards Harada. Bell wrote: 'Mr. Harada is personally known to Mr. Kanazawa and they meet fairly often on a friendly basis … I would simply say that he teaches an old fashioned system of karate … However, he is quite a nice man and is serious with his karate, as I believe are his students.'

In a reply letter of the 9th March, Kiernan noted that he had 'received some thirty plus applications to my advertisement and have arranged to have a meeting of all applicants on Friday, 18th March.' In his reply letter of the 17th March, Bell wrote that he regretted that Kanazawa could not visit the Portsmouth *dojo*, to which Kiernan had hoped to travel to, because the master's schedule had changed and he went to York instead. However, Mick Peachey visited Portsmouth in Kanazawa's absence.

Thirty-five prospective members attended the meeting and a five-man committee was elected with Kiernan as secretary. On the clubs inaugural training session, fifteen students partook. In his letter to Bell of the 3rd April, Kiernan noted: 'The present room that Mr. Tunnell and myself use is unfortunately too small for 15-20 people to practise in; we have therefore rented, on a temporary basis, a dance hall for one night a week, myself and Mr. Tunnell still keeping the old room for our own practice for a further five nights a week.' Kiernan then commented that he was trying to secure more permanent facilities through the Adult Further Education Services and planned to arrange press and television coverage. In addition, no doubt with the former in mind, he enquired of Kanazawa's availability in one or two months hence. As a postscript, Kiernan mentioned that Mick Peachey had been down again to give instruction to Mr. Tunnell and himself.

The final letter to survive from Kiernan is dated the 28th April 1966, where he noted that a large gymnasium with showers had been secured, and that 'numbers have settled down to nine members.' Mick Peachey was scheduled to travel down from London on the 7th May for a course in the Astor Institute between 2.30 p.m. and 5.30 p.m., and from 6.30 p.m. and 9.00 p.m. Kiernan proposed to have Peachey to teach one weekend a month. In the last of the Kiernan/Bell correspondence to have survived, Bell wrote on the 4th May, mentioning that Michael Randall would be accompanying Peachey. In this letter, he noted that Randall and Peachey had been on the Braden Beat television programme the previous month, and this presumably refers to the return visit mentioned on page 155 of Volume II.

Eight membership forms in all survive from the Plymouth *dojo* and the remaining seven will be presented in the usual format: Leslie Gaylard, 25, lorry driver (3.5.66); David Herrity, 22, pattern maker (28.3.66); Cyril James, 44, carpenter and joiner (—.5.66); Christopher Lake, 22, civil servant (28.3.66); David Streeter, 18, student (16.5.66); Kenneth Tunnell, 20, labourer (28.1.66); John Wilson, 21, cost clerk (18.4.66).

The BKF Bristol *dojo*, mentioned once in the BKF literature, is an error in the original, and should read 'Bath.' The Bath *dojo* was established and run by Brian Middleton, who applied to join the BKF on the 10th May 1965, aged seventeen. At the time of his application, this enterprising young man, who had interests in swimming, art and judo, was studying at Bath Technical College for his GCEs. Considerable correspondence between Middleton and Bell has survived, some of it interesting. The notion of commencing a Bath branch of the BKF arose in a letter, undated, but almost certainly December 1965, from Middleton to Bell. By July, members of the Sai Karate Club were training at the Bath and District Boys' Scouts headquarters, on Thursday evenings from 7.00 p.m. to 9.30 p.m. In a letter to Bell dated the 23rd September 1966, Middleton resigned as Area Officer (officially on the 6th October), unable to give the time, and, commenting that 'although it is only a small group, they are very

Brian Middleton – BKF Bath *dojo*, 1965

keen,' proposed that L. Vincent take over from him. In a reply letter dated the 24th September, Bell makes a rare reference to the disruption caused to the BKF as a result of major clubs leaving. He wrote: 'The BKF is in the process of complete re-organisation' – stark, unrevealing, and noteworthy.

What is unique about members of the Bath *dojo* at the time, at least in the author's knowledge, is that correspondence continues until January 1967, and the club did not leave the BKF the year other *dojos* did. Maybe they had a sense of loyalty, then again, perhaps, deep in the West Country, they hadn't heard. Arrangements for Ron Mills to travel to Bath to instruct were shelved due to the expense, and arrangements for members of the club to come to Upminster to train with Mills likewise fell through.

In a letter to Vincent dated the 14th December, we learn of the state the BKF found itself in at this time. Bell noted that Mills had resigned and that: 'Consequently we have now abandoned the karate system of Mr. Mills that we have been teaching for the last three months, namely, Shuko-kai, and we will revert to the old system we have taught for twelve [should read nine or ten] years, namely [the] Yoseikan style of [the] Shotokan school of which I am a 2nd Dan, and have taught for all these years ...' From this quote, one may infer that Bell was left bereft of senior Shotokan grades, and after what looks like a brief sojourn from the style, returned to the karate of Plee, Muchizuki and Murakami. In this letter, Bell noted an 'Area Officer from Merthyr Tydfil,' but nothing else is known about this individual or branch (that may never have got off the ground), which is beyond the time shutter of *Shotokan Dawn* in any case.

Vincent wrote to Bell on the 10th January 1967, replying to a lost letter from Bell dated the 8th January, where Bell apparently wrote that the BKF had amalgamated with the ABKA. Following on from this, Vincent wrote the potentially fateful words, for this is the last of his letters to have survived, 'Does this mean we are still affiliated to the JKA?'

In Bell's final letter to Vincent on the 17th January 1967, he notes two interesting points. Firstly, 'The BKF is still affiliated to the JKA and nothing has been received from the JKA headquarters withdrawing this authorised affiliation, and so you can take it that the BKF is still fully affiliated to the JKA until such time as the JKA itself rescinds this affiliation.' Secondly, and more surprisingly, 'As I already explained in my circular [now lost] our Technical Director is now Mr. T. Murakami, 5th Dan of the Yoseikan, who is resident in Paris, [and] who has consented to this office. We have requested him to come to England to teach as from April, which he has agreed to do, and further, he is attending the World Karate Congress. He will be conducting a one-week course in London in July, so you may now include his name on your letter headings.' This episode is a complete mystery and Murakami never did come to Britain again for the BKF.

The non-association with the JKA, officially notified or otherwise, soon caught up with Bell however. Mr. J. Willis of the Chelsea College Karate Club, London, for example, in an undated letter, writing in response to Bell's request for £25. 10. 0. for tuition, noted: 'It has been brought to our notice that the BKF is no longer affiliated to the JKA and was not at the time that six of our members applied and paid for licences. In view of this, we have deducted £9. 0. 0. from your fees.'

The BKF Bath *dojo* was indeed small, and only six members are recorded in all, along with Middleton, the remaining five will be presented in the usual format: Janet Brannen, 20, wages clerk (7.7.66); Peter Lythgoe, 21, student (1.6.66); David Parkes, 18, apprentice engineer (24.5.66); John Preston, 20, insurance manager (7.7.66); Larry Vincent, 18, cost clerk (15.2.66). In a letter to Bell by Vincent dated the 23rd November 1966, we learn that 'due to our rigorous training schedules, two of the six members decided to 'drop out.' The members in question are Miss. J. Brannen and Mr. D. Parkes.'

Similarly, in a letter of the 10th January, 1967, Vincent notes that Preston had resigned.

Bell was unable to remember what happened to the Poole, Portsmouth, Plymouth and Bath clubs, other than they all left the BKF.

Bell had no recollection of Birmingham or Glasgow BKF clubs, or of a C. Bauldry, who was supposedly attached to the latter. Apparently, a Kenneth Budge was planning to start a BKF Edinburgh branch in 1965, and perhaps that was where confusion arose with regard to the Scottish connection. There are no membership forms in existence for Edinburgh, so it is likely that the venture, at least in BKF terms, never got off the ground. In a letter of the 22nd July 1965, Budge wrote to Bell in response to a letter from Bell of the 22nd June. Budge was 'extremely disappointed that your [Bell's] previous promises have not been fulfilled,' and requested why his 'outfit and licence' had not materialised. In a reply of the 12th August, Bell apologised, but noted that both *gi* and licence had been sent two months previously. Bell was prepared to send replacements of both, hoping, 'we can be assured of your continued support and loyalty, and as a potential Area Officer you are invited to a special meeting.' A new licence exists for Budge.

A full list of BKF clubs at the time is given on Whitcher's Certificate of Proficiency (for the brown belt junior instructor status), dated the 3rd March 1966, on BKF letter-headed paper and signed by Bell and Kanazawa. Birmingham and Glasgow are not included on the list that runs down the left-hand side of the page. Clubs in Hull, Leeds, Leicester and Rainford are however listed, but no membership forms or documents of any kind have survived for any. There had been a BKF club in Leicester, but that ceased in 1963 of course, and a new branch is presumably being referred to. Perhaps the clubs at Hull and Leeds were university clubs as mentioned earlier, in which case they would have been formed in 1966 (they certainly weren't in the BKF on the 17th September 1964). A KUGB Leeds (non university) club was certainly up and running by March 1967. Later details of a Rainford club come from a write-up by Naylor (then 1st kyu) on page 4 of the October 1966 edition of *Karate News*. At the time of the piece it was noted that the club had 'four 5th kyu (purple) and a number of 6th kyu (green), 7th kyu (yellow) and 8th kyu (white).' The club had been running a year, and had practised Wado-ryu initially, before taking up Shotokan in February 1966. Training in October 1966 was on Tuesday and Thursday evenings, and Sunday mornings, and the *dojo*, which became based at the Lowe House Boys Club, St. Helens, had received instruction from Master Enoeda.

Page 176, line 17 – In a letter to Pinney, dated the 3rd November 1966, Bell wrote that: 'I would not renew his [Kanazawa's] work permit for an ensuing period, nor would I renew his contract ...' As the letter continues, we can clearly ascertain that Bell was unhappy.

Page 177, line 2 – The date of 12th May for Kanazawa's return is given in a letter Bell wrote to Gardner on the 24th February 1966. In two letters to Whittaker, the first, of the 16th March 1966, Bell noted that Kanazawa, 'returns to Japan in early May,' and in the second, of the 4th May, Bell commented that, 'Mr. Kanazawa will be returning to Japan on May 9th and Mr. Enoeda will take over from him in London,' coming down 'from Liverpool after the 13th May.' In a letter to Alan Marr, dated the 4th May, Bell again gives a date for Kanazawa's return as the 9th May, but in a letter to Ken Smith on the 19th May noted that Kanazawa 'left England on the 11th May.' In a letter to Grubb dated the 11th May, Bell wrote: 'Mr. Kanazawa had to finish work on the 18th April when his work permit finished and his legal contract with our Federation expired on the 28th April, and neither of these were renewed. Consequently, he was only staying on as a tourist and so left for Japan on the 11th May.' On the 3rd November 1966, Bell, in a letter to Swansea member, Pinney, noted Kanazawa returned to Japan on the 12th May.

    line 13 – Bell must have been expecting strong opposition for he wrote (letter now lost) of that year's Annual General Meeting to Whittaker. Whittaker replied on the 18th April, noting: 'I am very sorry indeed that it [the AGM] had to be declared void, and I'm disgusted that apparently serious karate students should conduct themselves in such a manner.' We do not know what Bell had written, of course.

Page 180, line 19 – In an 'Official Notice From the Secretary's Office,' we learn of a new BKF venture that, misinterpreted, caused Bell concern. Bell wrote: 'It has been brought to my notice that many members of the London *dojo* are of the opinion that the *dojo* at the Lyndhurst Hall will shortly be closing down and will be moved from there to Crystal Palace. I WISH TO MAKE IT QUITE CLEAR THAT THIS IS QUITE UNTRUE AND INCORRECT. I recently told members that the CCPR had offered us facilities at the Crystal Palace for a new *dojo* as well as our summer course, but at no time did I mention that the Crystal Palace would become our headquarters. Accordingly, the situation is that last week the director of the Crystal Palace offered the BKF facilities for holding classes in one of the smaller recreation halls at the National Recreation Centre ... and we agreed on Monday and Wednesday from 8-10 p.m. commencing the last week in April. This offer has been accepted but not yet finalised, with the objective being to have a *dojo* within the authority of the National governing body of sport in Britain, as well as working with the official organisation for sport. The object of this *dojo* would be to provide courses for novices and members on these two days to cater for people who live south of the Thames and counties around there. This *dojo* will be managed by myself with English instructors on both nights and with the Japanese instructor visiting periodically. Applications for membership of this new *dojo* will be considered in writing in strict rotation addressing full particulars to the National Secretary. The new London *dojo* will be a subsidiary to the main London *dojo* which will still be the Lyndhurst Hall, five nights weekly, continued permanently henceforth, and the Lyndhurst Hall will not be closed.' The Crystal Palace *dojo* never actually got off the ground, as Bell's letter to a Mr. Davies on the 11th May 1966 makes clear. Bell noted: 'I regret that I must cancel this arrangement due solely to the fact that due to reorganisation within our Federation, we no longer find it possible to provide qualified instructors on these two nights ...'

Bell's ambitious plans for BKF/JKA progress were mostly thwarted one way or another in 1966. Championships had been planned, and Bell had hoped to secure sponsorship from Japan Airlines for the 'first ever National Championships, finals and exhibitions [of karate] at the Main Area, Crystal Palace National Recreation Centre, on Saturday, 30th July 1966' (letter to Japan Airlines dated the 16th March 1966), for example. Bell had written the letter after he, Kanazawa and Enoeda had attended a conference of the CCPR on the 22nd February, the proposal apparently being made by the Technical Director of the CCPR. A Mr. A. Sladen, Publicity Manager for Japan Airlines, replied to Bell on the 17th March, noting that his company were already committed to sponsoring the British Judo Association that year, and suggested that Japan Airlines might be able to co-operate in other ways. In a letter to Sladen dated the 21st March, Bell quite understood Japan Airlines position, and had been unaware that the firm were sponsoring the BJA, and hoped that 'other ways' might include publicity for the championships. In a reply, and the final letter to have survived, dated the 22nd March, Sladen confirmed a time for meeting – 3.30 p.m. on Friday, 1st April.

In an earlier letter to a Mr. A. Grubb of the 24th February 1966, Bell, noting that he had secured Crystal Palace, wrote: 'At this tournament we are hoping to bring over the highest graded Japanese in Europe [Kase] and one from America [Nishiyama], to give the greatest exhibition of karate ever seen in Britain.' Bell also noted that the BKF Summer Course would also be held at Crystal Palace after the championships, and that the first inaugural meeting of the European Karate Federation would be held on the 1st August. Bell wondered whether the National Dairy Council would sponsor the said championships, but any thoughts of such were dashed in a reply letter to Bell on the 3rd March.

Bell appears to have first written to the organisers of The Dairy Festival on the 6th December 1965, and numerous letters followed between Bell and Grubb. Michael Barrington, a London *dojo* member, had written to Mr. David Bacon of the CCPR at 4, Whitehall Court, on the 10th December 1965, following a telephone conversation, regarding any help that might be available acquiring a central *dojo*. A reply letter on the 15th December was not overly helpful. As the Dairy Festival letters and Bell's subsequent letters to the CCPR (which, too, are numerous) are inter-linked, they will be dealt with together.

Bell wrote to Humphreys at the CCPR on the 4th March 1966, to apply for recognition as the 'official body for Shotokan karate for this country.' This is an important letter, Bell, wishing to work hand-in-hand with the CCPR 'to present Karate-do as a safe sport and a pleasurable hobby to be practised by young and old of both sexes, safely, and with enjoyment, and to free the name of karate from the tabs that have been placed on it as a killer sport, a super-normal art, and a lethal defensive Japanese blood sport, and in its place establish it as a form of physical education second to none, and on a par with and alongside judo and other sports.' Bell also wished to apply for a grant for a full-time National Coach, 'whom we preferably expect to be Japanese of the highest grade.'

Bell must have received a shock when, on the 17th March, Humphreys, replying to a lost letter from Bell of the 9th March, wrote informing Bell that a Mr. J. Summers, Chairman of the All British Karate-Do Association, whom Bell knew, would be involved, in some way that is unclear to the author, with the BKF application, though the ABKA had applied for representation (letter from E. Edwards, CCPR Acting Deputy Secretary, to Bell, dated 30th March). On the 21st March,

Bell wrote to Humphreys noting that he would be making an application to the secretary of the CCPR so that the BKF could be represented, and duly did so on the 28th March, in a letter to Mr. Justin Evans.

The demonstrations planned as part of The Dairy Festival, were throughout England and Wales. Bell was sent details on the 13th May to 'Britain's Eleventh Dairy Festival,' which was to be formally opened by The Rt. Hon. Enoch Powell, on Tuesday, 31st May 1966, at the Royal Exchange, London. On that day, there were to be demonstrations of gymnastics, fencing, golf, kendo, trampoline, weight-lifting, table tennis and karate. Whilst details are given for all other activities, under 'Karate-do', 'Details yet to be finalised' appears. Karate was scheduled for 1.00 p.m. that Tuesday and at the same time on the Friday. In a letter from Humphreys to Bell dated 13th May, we see that both Masters Kanazawa and Enoeda's names are given. On the May 1966, in 'Festival Review,' a 'Daily Mirror Extra,' karate is also mentioned. Some of the BKF branches were also scheduled to give demonstrations in their local areas.

From the tone of the letters that follow, and the cancellation by Bell of BKF involvement in the demonstrations, we see a glimpse of Bell's dissatisfaction and unhappiness with what was going on around him, and we see the beginnings of the BKF break-up more clearly. Kanazawa's work permit had expired, and the master was gone. In letters to Grubb on the 11th and 19th May, Bell wrote that Enoeda was unable to come down to London, and, in the later letter noted that 'because of this we have had to close down regular classes at our London headquarters as we have no resident instructor at this time and because our financial situation is extremely low … having expended £2,500 in the past year in keeping Mr. Kanazawa. Because of this shut down of classes, I have been unable to see, personally, hardly any of our instructors or senior members, even though I have written to six of them asking them to take part in this exhibition – only one has had the decency to reply by Monday last … As secretary of the Federation, I am powerless to do more, even though I have pleaded with the majority of London members to give at least one exhibition, none of them wish to offend Mr. ——- by taking part without his permission, for if they do he may view them with disfavour in the future, and it is the tradition in karate for the senior members only to take part in a public exhibition, under the style taught by the Japanese teacher, with his full consent. This seems to be the prime factor which I cannot overcome, and in fairness to all concerned, I must ask you to cancel our exhibitions, for I know of no way in which I can overcome these difficulties.

'I greatly regret having to do this after all the planning and agreements we have made in the past for your Festival, and it is a great disappointment to me especially, when I had such great hopes that much publicity and benefit would be derived from giving these exhibitions; this is indeed a sad loss to the BKF ... [and noted that another karate demonstration for the Eastern Counties Judo Tournament had to be cancelled as well] ... Since writing last I have had to cancel our championship at the Crystal Palace in July, since we do not even know if Enoeda will be in England at that time, for his parent organisation may recall him after his permit expires on the 2nd June.' Bell's letter of cancellation was to Davies on the 11th May 1966, noting: 'we have been unable to find a suitable sponsor to finance these championships as well as the departure of our resident Japanese teacher ...' It had been the intention, as proposed by Kanazawa and Enoeda, to have invited Nishiyama, Kase [as has been mentioned] and Shirai to these championships.

In reply to a lost letter of the 6th June from Humphreys, Bell, on the 8th June, noted that he was 'very surprised' that a member of the BKF had applied for representation on the London and South-east England standing conference of the CCPR. Bell replied that this individual 'was an ordinary member, under licence of the British Karate Federation, and he was recently dismissed from the Federation for conduct prejudicial to the interests of the Federation following a suspension last year with a warning of the Executive of the Federation, to curb his devious activities within the Federation, namely, trying to influence members of the Federation with courses of action liable to prejudice the policies of the Federation. He was severely reprimanded last year for attempting to interfere in the running of the Federation.
'This gentleman also owes the Federation monies for tuition in our London Branch which he had from our Japanese instructor on a three month course which he never paid for, between February and May this year ...' The two-page letter continues in the same vein.

line 38 – Thompson recalled: 'I got the impression that there was a lot of jostling going on about this time. I was not in the higher echelon at all; all I was interested in was my own club and training there. I had no higher aspirations then, or now. Not so it seemed with a lot of the others. Some of them were not working for some reason, and it seemed very likely to me that they were looking to make a living from karate one way or another. Maybe that was the reason that Mr. Bell sometimes acted the way he did. I give him his due, he did an awful lot to bring karate to this country in the form that he did ... Karate would have come to England whatever happened, but we have Mr. Bell to thank for establishing the Shotokan system here ... although in my opinion, in this country it is going in the wrong direction in a lot of ways. The only trouble with Mr. Bell was that he could not bear to share responsibility or listen to any other ideas but his own. At least that is the impression we got here up north. He was very clever in getting Mr. Kanazawa here on a contract that bound him to Mr. Bell personally. He wanted to be the only person to organise karate in any shape or form, and the sad thing is that if he had been a little more reasonable the breakaway may never have happened and he would have largely got what he wanted. That's my opinion anyway ...'

last line – As confirmation of this reversion, for example, in 1970, the BKF held a course in Yoseikan karate at the University of Keele on the 12th and 13th September: Saturday 10 a.m. – 12.30 p.m., 2.30 p.m. – 5.00 p.m.; Sunday, same times, followed by a grading 6.30 p.m. – 8.00 p.m. The fee for the course was £8. 8. 0., which included single accommodation and full board from Friday evening to late afternoon Sunday.

Page 181, line 12 – As an example to support rumours that the BKF no longer existed, Mr. N. Oswald wrote to Bell on the 14th June 1966: 'I have been informed by my branch secretary (Portsmouth), that the BKF has been disbanded and that a new karate federation has been formed, which is now officiated by a committee of which you have no part. I have been told that my BKF licence is now of no further use, so under the circumstances, I wish you to return the £5. 0. 0. to me so I may join the new karate federation and also purchase a suit from them.'

One imagines that, in response to such letters, Bell wrote the following undated letter: 'It has been brought to my notice by various members, that there is a rumour circulating among the branches that the BKF has gone into liquidation and broken up and that I have retired from karate. I wish to assure you that this is completely untrue, and the BKF is still active and continuing to function as always and growing stronger every day, and will soon be a part of a vast new European organization with Japanese backing with our own resident Japanese master.

'The BKF has been put on a sound legalised footing with properly audited accounts. The London *dojo* is still functioning properly with new instructors. I wish to state clearly that any of the old branches affiliated to the BKF may remain so and continue to enjoy the privileges of affiliation. But note that any member or branch who has seen fit to be disloyal or leave the BKF to join the breakaway movement will no longer be allowed to continue within the framework of our Federation. Kindly also observe, that should any member of a branch or any person, for that matter, interfere with the working of the BKF or do anything to damage its reputation or to intimidate its members, full legal action will be pursued against that member at once.

'We hope we may continue with your further support and loyalty for the development of karate as an organised federation under experienced leaders.'

Page 185, line 6 – Thompson continued: 'I remember blotting my copy book with the KUGB when it was first formed. Old habits die hard and we were in the habit of booking Mr. Kanazawa direct at this time and the last time we did this he put off a booking elsewhere to come to York. I got a ticking off from Terry Heaton for this and was forcibly told that all bookings must go through the KUGB bookings secretary, or whatever he called himself. Okay, I deserved the wigging I suppose, but it came hard, learning that our 'special relationship' had gone down the nick ... [complaining about perceived interference and bureaucracy during 'teething trouble mainly'] I had been running my club long before some of these 'officials' had even heard of karate [and] I felt a bit put out at times.'

line 17 – Leslie Hart, 21, insurance clerk, applied for BKF membership on the 3rd April 1961. On his application form, he declared his hobbies as being judo, kendo and quarter staff fencing. He graded to a judo black belt in 1960 under Kawaishi of the Kodokwai.

line 32 – However, David Hartland, a twenty-four-year-old building technician from Sparkhill, Birmingham, applied for BKF membership on the 5th October 1965.

Page 186, line 3 – On his BKF application form, Heaton makes no reference to being in the parachute regiment, nor of being a judo *Shodan* – but then there is no reason why he should have. He noted that he had been in the army for seven years (demobilisation in 1950) and held the rank of sergeant and, as a member of the BJA, listed judo as a 'sport played.' On the later BKF application for membership form, there were no questions asking about Armed Services' record, or judo grades held.

Bell remembered Heaton so: "He was an intelligent man, but I found him very spurious. I never knew how I stood with him. Whilst I can't say I warmed to him, he was genuine about wanting to start Shotokan in Manchester in 1964."

line 6 – Stanley Dalton, of the York *dojo*, and a solicitor by profession, became the first Chairman.

line 7 – Kanazawa's address in March 1967 was: 17 Collingham Place, London, SW5.

Page 190, line 14 – The 'individual' was Anthony Creamer; the 'man' was Andrew Allan.

line 17 – Both men were twenty years old and employed as waiters. In an article entitled, 'First Karate Killer Jailed,' by Arnold Latcham, from an unknown newspaper, we learn that the judge, Mr. Justice Glyn-Jones, was 'horrified at the suddenness and expertise with which Creamer [a slightly-built man] killed.' Creamer noted that Allan had made improper advances to his sixteen-year-old brother and a fight started. Creamer continued: 'He tried to push me out of the window [of his flat in Clanicarde Gardens, Notting Hill Gate]. I dealt him seven karate blows in self-defence. I went berserk. I gave him a flying kick to the throat. I smashed him on top of the head. I hit him on the jaw with my elbow, and used my fingers in his stomach.' Allan's cause of death is reported as being due to six broken ribs and a torn liver, lungs and voice box. In another report by Harry Longmuir that appeared on page 7 of the *Daily Mail* (Wednesday, 26th October), where Creamer is described as being a kitchen porter, and Allan, a barman, it was noted that a post-mortem had revealed 'six fractured ribs, two ruptures of the liver, two fractures of the voice box and considerable bruising of the lung.' In a boxed interlude in this piece it is recorded that, 'The British Karate Federation does not accept anyone who it thinks might use the skill for criminal purposes.'

The above *Daily Mail* report is accompanied by a picture of Master Suzuki, and another article entitled: 'To the Professor From Japan Karate has Become a Way of Life – The Cult,' by John Spicer, it notes that, 'Ten years ago there was only one karate club in Britain. Today, there are more than one hundred, with a total membership of ten thousand.'

Another article on page 8 of *The Sunday Times* (30th October 1966), entitled, 'Karate – the Crunch,' by an unknown author, adds to the debate. However, the BKF is mentioned: 'And British karate students who cannot work off all their aggressions on the mat can always turn to karate politics, where no fewer than four separate organisations are jockeying for influence. The oldest, the British Karate Federation, is run by a ex-RAF PT instructor, Vernon Bell, who was operating clandestine classes in Essex long before James Bond was translated into celluloid.' Bell, in fact wrote a four-page letter to *The Sunday Times* with regard to the BKF's inclusion in the piece, and received a reply on the 14th December by James Dow, managing editor. Bell's letter contains some pertinent and historically interesting information. Bell took umbrage with the word 'clandestine' that was used, noting that BKF training and 'membership of my clubs ... [was] open to the general public after screening and investigation ...' Bell continues that he brought karate to Britain in April 1957, 'having studied in Paris for two years under the then leading experts ...' Bell, in 2003, maintained that he started training with Plee in 1955, and this letter, being much closer in time, tends to back this argument up (though there is no documentary evidence to support this earlier date {see the author's, *Shotokan Horizon*}). The article also erroneously noted that the ABKA split from the BKF, and Bell was at pains to point out that this was not the case. We also learn that 'rebellious London members formed themselves into a group ... and they brought Kanazawa back on June 10th from Belgium, where he was staying with another Japanese, Mr. Kase.' Bell also requested that the corrections be published.

A later article in *Parade* (3rd December, 1966, pages 9, 11-12) entitled, 'Karate – Menace or Sport?' by W.N. Dover, refers to the Creamer case and contains some 'interesting' information. For example, Dover notes that, 'there are cases of quarrels between Japanese troops in which serious injury and death resulted from karate fighting.' In conclusion, it was suggested that, 'The danger to the public from karate in the hands of the wrong people is therefore probably exaggerated. After all, both boxing and wrestling provide techniques of potential danger to an unskilled adversary. But assaults by boxers and wrestlers are virtually unknown.' The BKF is mentioned in the article, as is the 'Karate Union,' presumably referring to the KUGB. A photograph of Ray Fuller breaking two, one-inch wooden boards held by Harper and Chisholm, with a *gyaku-zuki,* taken from the Pathé Pictorial film noted on pages 299-300 of Volume I of *Shotokan Dawn* is also shown.

line 21 – Bell actually wrote to Braine on the 3rd November 1966, in the form of a three-page letter, on the organisation of karate in Great Britain, and offering his advice should Braine require it. Braine replied from the House of Commons on the 10th

November 1966. Bell wrote again on the 15th November noting that he was 'very pleased to hear that this information is both of interest and assistance to you.' In this letter, Bell offered his help to Braine once more, and seemed to support an inquiry. Braine replied to Bell on the 21st November, remarking that the Home Office had agreed to make some enquiries into karate, and felt sure 'that the Home Secretary will be pleased to receive any views that the bone-fide clubs and experienced persons such as yourself might care to express.' Apparently, from what the author can discern, a number of questions were asked in the House of Commons on the 17th November 1966, and Braine sent Bell a copy of these. Essentially, Braine and a Mr. Rhodes, who wanted to draw attention to the fact that karate clubs were in the North of England and anyone could seemingly join them, received information from a Mr. Taverne that inquiries into karate were being made.

line 23 – Following on from this murder, Ian MacLaren, the 'public relations officer to the York Shotokan Karate Club,' was interviewed by an unknown reporter in an unknown Yorkshire paper. The article, entitled, 'Dangerous in Wrong Hands,' is, basically, a reaffirmation of what karate really is. Interestingly, in contrast to a previously recorded report concerning the cost of having a Japanese karate instructor at the club, the reporter noted: 'Kanazawa ... comes to York for a week several times each year. It costs the club about £70.'

Bell, for one, wanted to correct the misconception about karate as a consequence of the Creamer trial. In an article on page 17 of *The Recorder* entitled, 'And Now the Case for Karate: Black-Belt Against a Ban On It' (1st December 1966), and with the caption to the piece's accompanying photograph of Bell and Mills reading '... anxious to keep their sport alive,' the content and intent of the report by Ian Cole is obvious.

line 26 – In a letter of the 3rd November 1966, to Swansea member, Pinney, Bell provides us with a date for Kanazawa's return to England – 11th June.

Page 191, line 39 – Garth Hall was located in Granville Road, the relevant section of which has now become Mortimer Close. Students who trained at Garth Hall sometimes went around to Dr. Gould's house, as did both Master Kanazawa and Enoeda. Nick Adamou recalled attending a party there, and Kanazawa and Enoeda trying out a *makiwara* in the garden.

A side view of Garth Hall (2002), (II/192)

Page 192, line 16 – Nick Adamou remembered the demonstration of *Kanku-Dai* that Kanazawa gave when the Garth Hall *dojo* in Childs Hill was being established. He recalled: '[The *kata*] was, of course, phenomenal in terms of speed, power, artistry, and so on. When he [Kanazawa] had finished it, he walked slowly and majestically out of the *dojo*, through a partition at the back of the *dojo* to where Enoeda *Sensei* was getting ready for his *kata*. The partition wasn't fully closed in the middle, so I was able to see Kanazawa *Sensei* crouch down close to Enoeda *Sensei* and in a half laughing, whilst gasping and shattered manner, discussed things about his performance. I was shocked to catch a glimpse of Kanazawa *Sensei* [like this]. However, minutes after, I deduced that if you are constantly teaching and travelling, and then every now and then have to go into 'overdrive', like he had just done, then it's only normal that you'd be shattered.'

Page 196, line 2 – In the letter to the editor of *The Sunday Times* already referred to, Bell noted: 'I would add that the Karate Union has several times in the past month or so offered me positions as Assistant Secretary, Southern Area Officer, etc, to the Union, none of which I have accepted ...'

Heaton applied to join the BKF on the 20th November 1964, and is

Terry Heaton – Manchester *dojo*, 1964

recorded as having graded to 8th kyu on 1st January 1965, and to 7th kyu on the 31st March, both under Bell. Then, on the 11th December 1965, Heaton graded to 6th kyu, and on the 20th March 1966, to 5th kyu, both under Master Enoeda, all of which has been noted previously. It may seem odd therefore, that on page 5 of the October 1966 edition of the *Karate News: the official news magazine of the Karate Union of Great Britain,* Heaton is cited as being a 1st Dan. Perhaps it referred to his judo grade (awarded in 1949)? Maybe it was an honorary karate award, for it seems somewhat incredulous that he might have achieved five grades in seven months (and a black belt in less than two years), for he was, by all accounts, of moderate technical ability. If it referred to a karate grade, then perhaps it was an error, but one would have thought that unlikely, especially when, in 1966, KUGB *Shodans* were so very few in number, and such a glaring error in what is believe to be the first edition of the magazine – when great care might be expected, not least by the editor of the magazine, Peter Maude, who was a member of the Manchester *dojo* – would surely have been striking to a proof reader in a publication of only twelve pages.

In the March 1967 edition of the same magazine (which is likely to be issue 3), a profile of Heaton is given by John Boughen, where it is noted that Heaton 'is a First Dan judo as well as karate.' An accompanying photograph records: 'Karate Union Secretary Terry

Heaton, *Shodan* ...' On page 3 of Number 11 of *Karate* magazine (1969), Heaton writes an article entitled, 'Hard Work, It's the Only Way,' lauding the virtues of achieving a black belt through hard training, noting that to achieve Dan status, 'the only way is to take lessons under a competent instructor for a period of from three to five years.' His grade is given as 2nd Dan at this stage, which is reaffirmed in another photograph caption. The author attempted to resolve any ambiguity regarding Heaton's Dan status, but without success.

Page 197, last paragraph – Gordon Thompson shared Bell's final comments. In a private communication to the author (17th September, 2002), he noted: 'What is missing is the old pioneering spirit. We were doing something new, setting up an unknown discipline, making our own way and learning by our mistakes. It is this spirit which is gone … [Today] there are no questions to answer. The new student has a programme laid out for him and he knows where he is going and how he is expected to progress. We didn't have this; we had to make our own way and it was this that was so exciting.'

POSTSCRIPT

Master Enoeda died of stomach cancer on the 29th March 2003, after complications set in whilst receiving treatment in Japan. He was sixty-seven years old. He is survived by his wife, Reiko, and their two children, Daisuke and Maya (see *The Times* obituary {page 31, 9th April 2003}).

Vernon Bell died on the 27th February 2004, at Newham Hospital, Plaistow, London, after being rushed there by ambulance. The cause of death, as certified by Dr. T. M. Kiyani, was metastatic prostate carcinoma and prostate carcinoma. Bell's death was registered by his son, Graham V. Bell, on the 1st March 2004, and gave his father's occupation as 'hypnotherapist (retired).' Bell, who was eighty-one at the time of death, had given a courageous battle against prostate cancer and its secondary complications for a number of years. His body gave

The end of an era. Vernon Bell's gravestone, recording that he was founder of the British karate movement.

up, but his spirit never gave up. He married three times (Rita Meeson and Pauline Whitehead having already been alluded to in *Shotokan Dawn*, he also married Margaret C. Pratt in 1978) and was divorced three times. He is survived by three sons and one daughter (a further two sons having died). Bell's obituary was published on page 28 of

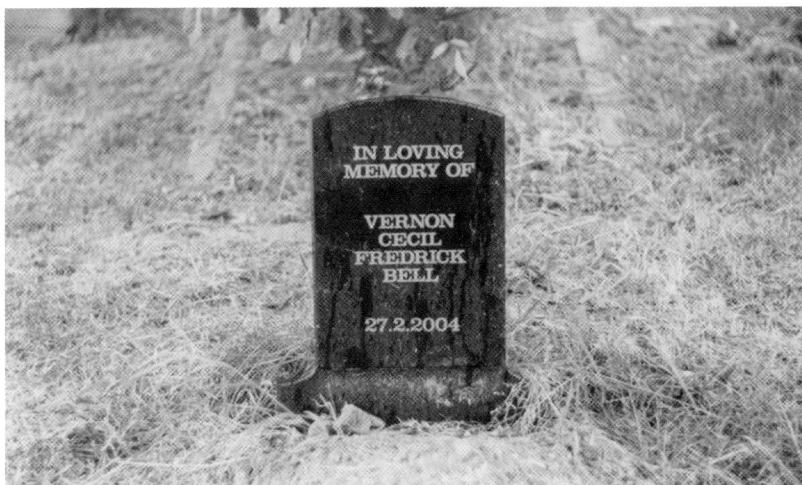

The headstone that marks Bell's actual place of burial

The Times, on the 8th March 2004 (page 56 of *The Times* compact edition) with the present author supplying the details. His funeral was held that same day, at 11.00 a.m., at West Ham Cemetery, London, E7, where he was buried, in his *gi*, close to one of his sons. Some sixty mourners were in attendance, including former loyal BKF *karateka* Terry Wingrove, who read the eulogy, Michael Randall and William Mannion. The author was also present. For those readers wishing to pay their respects, Bell's grave lies some fifty metres away, and directly in line with, the cemetery's chapel entrance. The gravestone, that records that Bell was the founder of the British karate movement, does not actually mark the exact spot of his place of burial, which is slightly before this grave and to the right, when facing the gravestone.

Master Kase suffered a major heart attack in 1999, and despite resuming training (giving a come-back course in Paris in February 2000) he never really fully recovered. On the 24th November 2004, he was fatally struck down by another heart attack at his home in Paris. He was seventy-five years old. He left the JKA and formed the World Karate Shotokan Academy with Shirai in 1989, before the Shotokan Ryu Kase Ha. He is survived by his wife, Cheiko, and their daughters, one of whom is named Sachiko. Kase was cremated on the 30th November 2004, at Père Lachaise, Paris.

APPENDIX I

UNCLASSIFIED BKF MEMBERS

A document entitled, 'A.R.F Renewals' [Annual Registration Fee Renewals] has been discovered that lists licence renewals for twenty-eight BKF members unrecorded in *Shotokan Dawn* or in this supplement. Names will be given in the order they appear in the manuscript, along with their dates of renewal. *It is likely that most, if not all, are not renewals at all, but first-time licensees.* All unrecorded names, bar one, are known to be novices, to 'Kennedy.' It is unknown which *dojos* these students were aligned too, hence 'unclassified.' Their ages, sex and social class are also unknown. The manuscript begins entries at No. 1, proceeds to No. 4, then there is a gap to 42E, with entries known to be lost (Bell). If a name appears twice, the earlier date is given. There are 567 entries in the original. The names are as follows:

Walker, A. (01/06/61), Snow, E.* (01/01/61), Alvis, T. (01/07/61), Page, M. (01/07/61), Howlett, T. (15/01/62), Moore, A. (18/01/62), Hughes, T. (15/02/62), Farrar, R. (01/01/62), Kennedy, G. (01/01/63), Atkins, B. (11/01/63), Williams, C. (01/01/63), Chretian, T. (27/01/63), Stopler, M. (24/01/63), Smith, F. (01/01/63), Cartek, J. (01/01/63), King, M. (04/03/63), Glasgow, J. (25/03/63), Newman, P. (26/03/63), Shepherd, M. (01/01/63), Hicks, P. (24/03/63), Hannah, T. (09/04/63), Shear, S. (05/08/63), Evans, F. (07/08/63), Berg, J. (18/09/63), Stillman, R. (09/09/63), Cronk, D. (19/09/63), O'Keefe, C. (01/10/63), Perry, G. (16/09/63).

* Snow was registered as a 5th kyu.

APPENDIX II

THE BKF REGISTER OF ENQUIRIES

The *BKF Register of Enquiries* is an interesting document. Compiled over nearly seven and a half years (first entry 26th July 1957; last entry undated, but probably February 1964) by Vernon Bell's father, contains 410 entries, under the following headings: Number, Date, Name, Initials, Address, Judo Club (if any), Grade, Graded by, Date, Where Heard of BKF, Source of Enquiry, Reason for Enquiry, Replied to Date, Literature Sent, Acknowledgement Received, BKF Membership, Remarks. A table of results provides us with the following information:

TABLE 1

THE BKF REGISTER OF ENQUIRIES

YEAR[1]	ENQUIRIES[2] 1 2 3 4	JUDOKA[3]	GRADED[4,5]	TOTAL	JOINED BKF	%JOIN	CUM%[6]
1957	1 12 3 0	2	2	16[7]	1	6.3	6.3
1958	0 3 1 2	4	4	6	0	0	4.6
1959	2 9 9 19	14	2	39	3	7.7	6.6
1960	2 7 7 12	11	5	28	2	7.1	6.7
1961	0 10 13 62	23	17	85	12	14.1	10.3
1962	1 9 18 65	21	8	93	21	22.6	14.6
1963	0 11 27 72	12	7	110	14	12.7	14.1
1964	0 1 7 25	3	1	33[8]	5	15.2	14.2

NOTES:

1 In the few cases where the year is unknown, then year of reply is given.
2 Enquiry categories are as a result of: 1 – karate demonstration live or on television; 2 – book, article, advert, leaflet, library; 3 – recommendation by persons or martial arts' associations; 4 – unknown.
3 This merely refers to those who declared that they practised judo in their enquiry letter. It is known that some applicants who went on to become BKF members had studied judo, but made no mention of it in their initial enquiry.
4 This merely refers to those *judoka* who declared a grade in their enquiry letter. Principal, Instructor and Part-time Instructor are counted as 'graded' when grades are unknown; 'Secretary' is not classed as graded.
5 A number of Dan grade *judoka* made enquires to the BKF. The first in the Enquiry Register is C. Allen, AJA *Shodan,* on the 26th October 1958; then, T. Edmunds, *Nidan,* 6th August 1959; J.W. Dickie, AJA *Nidan,* early 1960 (under reason for enquiry is written, 'establish

karate in Scotland'); W. Gray, *Nidan*, end of 1960; J. Roberts, AJA *Nidan*, 16th December 1960; T. Alvis, *Shodan*, 10th July 1961; M. Smith, USAF *Nidan*, summer 1961; R. Butterworth, BJA *Shodan*, 15th September 1961; S. Aitken, *Nidan*, 13th May 1962; J. Brown, *Shodan*, 18th August 1962; D. Gilbert, *Shodan*, late summer, 1962; T. Sutherland, BJC *Shodan*, January 1964. Only Alvis appears to have joined the BKF.

6   Cumulative percentage who joined the BKF.
7   Under 'Remarks', it appears that six of these potential members were rejected in 1957.
8   Only two months of 1964 were included before the register was discontinued.

Additional notes:
1) A number of individuals wrote twice or more, these are only referenced once.
2) Geographically, enquiries effectively spanned the length and breadth of England, and a few came from Scotland and Ireland. One each came from South Africa, British Columbia, New York and Germany.
3) In the summer of 1962, Bell received a letter from a G. Smith of Kirkstall, who appears to have trained at the 'Kirkstall Karate Club,' and was 'instructing at three clubs.' Nothing else is known about this individual or the clubs, none of which were registered with the BKF.
4) In early September 1963, Bell received a letter from an I. Hiyazi, of London, N.5, and an appointment was made for 9.15 p.m. on the 10th September 1963. Nothing else is known about Hiyazi or what transpired as a result of the meeting.

GRAPH 1

A BAR GRAPH SHOWING THE ORIGIN OF RECORDED BKF ENQUIRIES
BY YEAR

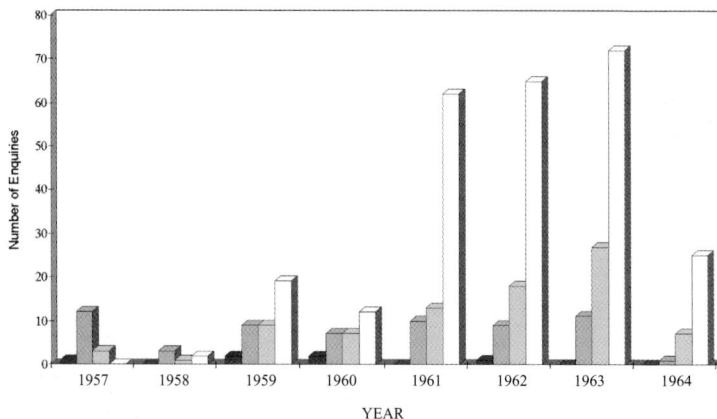

KEY:

Black = Visual: karate demonstration live, or on television

Dark grey = Literary: book, article, advert, leaflet, library

Light grey = Personal: recommendation by persons or martial arts' associations

White = Unknown

GRAPH 2

A BAR GRAPH SHOWING THE NUMBER OF RECORDED BKF ENQUIRIES BY
YEAR, AND THE NUMBER OF ENQUIREES WHO BECAME BKF MEMBERS

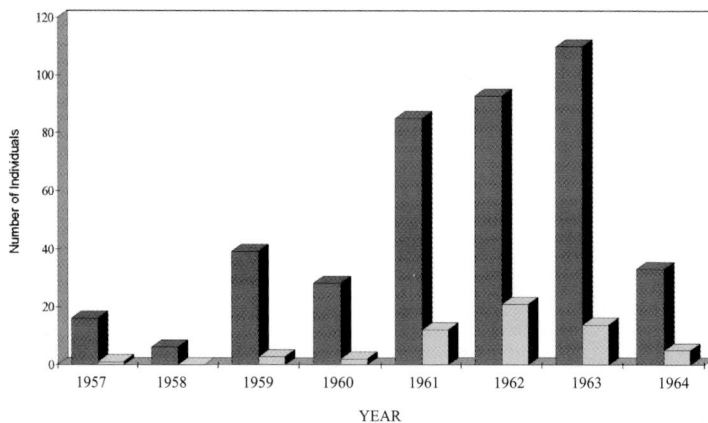

KEY:

Dark grey = Nō. of recorded BKF enquiries.

Light grey = Nō. who became BKF members

APPENDIX III

THE NUMBER OF STUDENTS JOINING THE BKF BY YEAR (excluding Eire)

GRAPH 3

A BAR GRAPH SHOWING THE NUMBER OF STUDENTS JOINING THE BKF BY YEAR (excluding Eire)

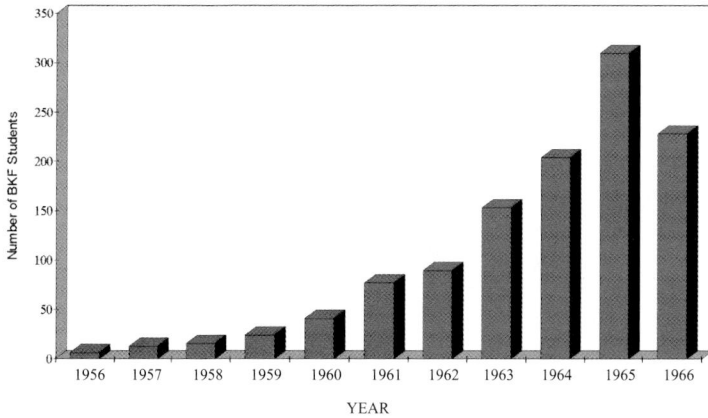

	1956	1957	1958	1959	1960	1961	1962	1963	1964	1965	1966
Male (Nō. 1143)	6	10	16	24	41	76	90	152	198	305	225
Female (Nō. 17)	0	2	0	0	0	1	0	1	6	4	3
Total (Nō. 1160)	6	12	16	24	41	77	90	153	204	309	228

NOTES:
1) Some of the very earliest students did not complete BKF membership forms, but ju-jitsu and judo forms. These few students trained in BKF karate, as it were, before the BKF was actually officially formed in 1957.
2) Dated membership forms/renewal of licence data are included. The year of 'renewal' is included (see above under 'Unclassified Individuals').
3) Records are known to be incomplete for 1965 and 1966.
4) All BKF female members are believed known (Bell), therefore undeclared are treated as male.
5) 98.3% of BKF application for membership forms are dated.

APPENDIX IV

BKF DOJO NUMBERS IN BRITAIN (1956[1]-1966)

GRAPH 4

A BAR GRAPH SHOWING BKF DOJO NUMBERS IN BRITAIN (1956-1966)

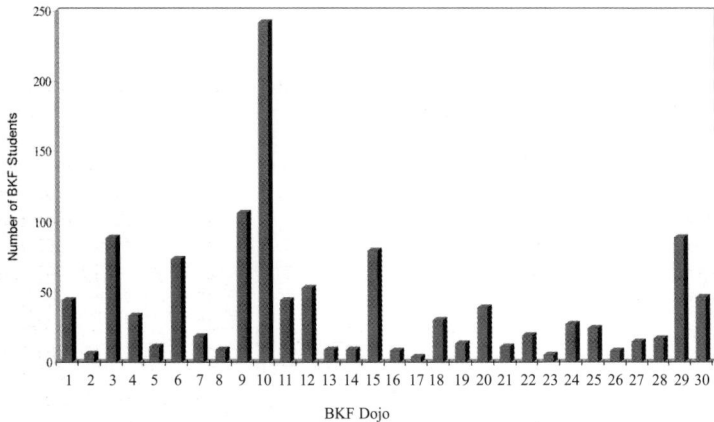

Key to BKF Dojos:

1 - Aberdeen	12 - Middlesbrough	23 - Stoke A
2 - Bath	13 - Mullards	24 - Stoke B
3 - Blackpool	14 - Newport	25 - Sunderland
4 - Bradford	15 - Nottingham	26 - Swansea
5 - Chiswick	16 - Plymouth	27 - USAF Denham
6 - Dundee	17 - Poole	28 - USAF High
7 - Hornchurch	18 - Portsmouth	Wycombe
8 - Leicester	19 - RAF Scampton	29 - York
9 - Liverpool	20 - Rotherham	30 - Unknown affiliation
10 - London/Upminster	21 - Saltcoats	
11 - Manchester	22 - 2nd Parachute Reg.	

NOTE:

1) Some of the very earliest students did not complete BKF membership forms, but ju-jitsu and judo forms. These few students trained in BKF karate, as it were, before the BKF was actually officially formed in 1957. Such students trained in Hornchurch.

APPENDIX V

THE AGE OF BKF KARATEKA AT THE TIME OF THEIR APPLICATION (excluding Eire)

TABLE 2

THE AGE OF BKF KARATEKA AT THE TIME OF THEIR APPLICATION (excluding Eire)

Dojo	N	% known[1]	Av. age[2]	SD[3]	Youngest	Oldest	Years covered
Aberdeen	42	95.5	22.2	6.6	15	39	1963-1966
Bath	5	100	18.8	1.6	17	21	1965-1966
Bath (all)[4]	6	100	19.0	1.6	17	21	1965-1966
Blackpool	68	76.4	23.6	7.2	15	46	1962-1966
Blackpool (all)	71	79.8	23.4	7.1	15	46	1962-1966
Bradford	27	81.8	24.2	6.3	17	40	1963-1966
Chiswick	7	63.6	25.0	3.5	19	31	1966
Dundee	61	83.6	24.0	7.2	14	45	1964-1965
Hornchurch	8	44.4	25.9	5.6	18	34	1956-1957
Leicester	9	100	23.1	6.1	16	32	1962-1963
Liverpool	76	70.8	23.4	6.9	13	40	1959-1965
London/Upminster	180	74.4	26.2	7.8	14	59	1958-1966
London/Upminster (all)	183	75.6	26.3	7.8	14	59	1958-1966
Manchester	41	93.2	23.4	6.2	16	50	1964-1966
Manchester (all)	43	97.7	23.4	6.3	16	50	1964-1966
Middlesbrough	48	90.6	22.2	6.7	15	41	1960-1964
Middlesbrough (all)	52	98.1	21.8	6.6	14	41	1960-1964
Mullards	9	100	24.6	3.0	19	33	1964-1965
Newport	9	100	25.9	4.3	21	33	1963-1964
Nottingham	78	98.7	25.3	7.8	14	48	1965-1966
Plymouth	8	100	24.3	8.2	18	44	1966
Poole	3	75.0	29.3	3.2	27	33	1966
Portsmouth	30	100	26.0	6.7	18	43	1964-1966
RAF Scampton	13	100	25.2	5.2	17	33	1961-1962
Rotherham	37	94.9	21.9	4.2	15	36	1964-1966
Saltcoats	11	100	23.9	6.4	17	40	1961-1963
2nd Parachute Reg.	19	100	21.8	2.3	18	26	1963
Stoke A	5	100	20.4	4.3	17	26	1960-1961
Stoke B	25	92.6	27.8	9.3	15	47	1966
Stoke B (all)	26	96.3	27.9	9.1	15	47	1966
Sunderland	23	95.8	24.1	7.7	17	42	1966
Swansea	8	100	18.0	1.4	17	21	1965-1966

Table continued

TABLE 2 - *continued*

Dojo	N	% known[1]	Av. age[2]	SD[3]	Youngest	Oldest	Years covered
USAF Denham	14	93.3	23.4	5.3	14	32	1961-1962
USAF High Wycombe	14	82.4	23.0	5.3	17	33	1962
York	77	86.5	23.4	7.2	15	47	1961-1966
York (all)	78	87.6	23.4	7.2	15	47	1961-1966
Unknown affiliation	10	17.5	26.8	8.2	19	45	1959-1965
Males only	965	82.1	24.2	7.1	13	59	1956-1966
Females only	15	88.2	21.8	7.0	14	43	1961-1966
Total	980	82.2	24.2	7.1	13	59	1956-1966

NOTES:

1) % known = percentage of ages known for each *dojo*
2) Av. Age = average age
3) SD = standard deviation
4) Data is presented for each *dojo* for males only, unless females also trained, in which 'all' covers both male and female. All BKF female members are believed known (Bell), therefore undeclared are treated as male.

The ages of 83% of British BKF students are known.

APPENDIX VI

THE SOCIAL CLASS OF BKF KARATEKA AT THE TIME OF THEIR APPLICATION (excluding Eire)

GRAPH 5

A BAR GRAPH SHOWING THE SOCIAL CLASS OF BKF KARATEKA AT THE TIME OF THEIR APPLICATION (excluding Eire)

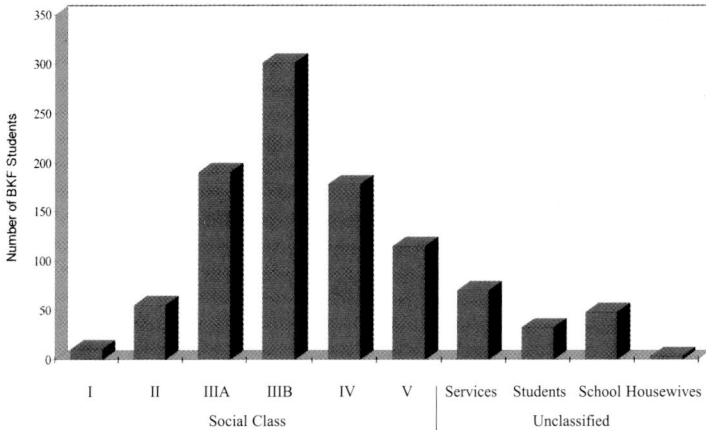

	I	II	IIIA	IIIB	IV	V	Services	Students	School	Housewives
Nō.	10	55	190	300	178	115	70	32	48	3

Total: 1001

NOTES:

1) The UK Registrar General's Classification of Social Class based on occupation at the time, was as follows: Group I – professional (doctors, lawyers, academics, etc); Group II – intermediate (managerial and lower professional - managers, teachers, etc); Group IIIA – skilled occupations, non-manual; Group IIIB – skilled occupations, manual; Group IV – partly skilled, and, Group V – unskilled. The Registrar General's classification, with minor alterations, was in existence for eighty-nine years, to be replaced by the National Statistics Socio-Economic Classification (NS-SEC) in 2001. Many BKF students were manual apprentices, and they have been classed as IIIB, as though they completed their apprenticeships.

2) The Armed Services, students in Higher Education (18 yrs and over), school pupils (18 yrs and under) and housewives, are not classifiable.

3) 82.4% of BKF application for membership forms state occupation.

4) 2% of BKF application forms for London/Upminster members whose occupation is not stated, Bell recalled their occupation from memory – therefore, 84.4% of occupations are included above.

APPENDIX VII

SCHEDULE AND INVENTORY OF ALL BRITISH KARATE FEDERATION PROPERTY, EQUIPMENT AND DOCUMENTS, AS AT 17th SEPTEMBER, 1964

'One filing cabinet marked '2' in the front room, 91 Perrymans Farm Road, Newbury Park.

Top Drawer: Contents

1. All Branch Files containing branch records, members' details, and all correspondence with Branch Officers (London, Ayrshire, Aberdeen, Blackpool, Dundee, Liverpool A-G, H-M, N-Z, Middlesborough A-G, H-Z, Middlesborough correspondence, American Branch, Mullards Electric, Notts, Rotherham, Newport, York branches).
   Sundry Files: dismissed members, associates, sundry members, files [of] members 1962/63, associates 1962/63, associate members expired, full members expired.

Second Drawer: Contents

1. Enquiries 1-241, enquiries 242-499, enquiries 500 to date
2. American book lists
3. Sundry course files
4. Grading record
5. Correspondence L.J.S. [Seydel] and E.J. Harrison
6. Old Summer Course leaflets
7. J. Milom order records [Manchester supplier of *gis* to the BKF – file lost]
8. Course enquiries
9. Displays
10. Bills and receipts
11. Typist's time sheets
12. Badges and trophies etc.
13. *Budo Presse* file
14. Halls and *dojos*
15. Press articles
16. Karate *Shodan* course records
17. H.D. Plee and Foulsham records
18. International Karate Federation
19. Unqualified experts record
20. B.J.A. correspondence
21. US Karate Association correspondence
22. Sundry American bodies
23. Paja *dojo* [a *dojo* in India, according to Bell – file lost]

24. French Federation of Karate correspondence
25. E.K.F.
26. Mochizuki and Delcourt
27. Ng-Tat-Man
28. J.K.A. official file
29. German Karate Federation
30. Federation of Vietnam
31. Canadian Karate Association
32. Belgian Karate Federation
33. Discontinued braches: USAF High Wycombe, Lincoln, 2nd Parachute, USAF Durham [should read 'Denham'], Leicester, Eire A-H, I-Z
34. Payments book
35. London *dojo* fees
36. J.K.A. orders
37. Current bank statement, bank paying-in book, two leather folders containing bank statements for previous five years, two paying-in books
38. Official grading records
39. Current correspondence awaiting attention
40. Current membership awaiting licences
41. Current course enrolment
42. Notices [for] course enrolments

Third Drawer: Contents
1. *Karate* by Nishiyama and Brown
2. *Elementary Anatomy and Physiology*
3. *Karate-Do* by Funakoshi
4. *Fighting Arts of the Orient* by Gilbey
5. *Arwrology* by Perrigard
6. *Kill or Get Killed*
7. *Fighting Arts of the Orient* by Paul Pung
8. *Kempo Karate* by Ed Parker
9. *Kungu-Fu Karate* by Lee
10. *Chinese Karate Kung-Fu* by Wong (two copies)
11. *Karate Self-Defence* by Nakayama
12. *Self-Defence and Attack* by Royman
13. *Karate* by Jurgen Seydel – three volumes: Volumes I and II in translation. Note – Volume III in process of translation in Germany by Miss Bauer
14. *Karate-Do* by Reikichi – four volumes
15. *Zen Combat* by Gluck
16. Film: *Aikido*
17. Film: *Techniques of Karate* – Reels 1,2,3 (at York), 4,5,6
18. Two black karate belts
19. *Skill* magazine – 26 [copies]. According to Bell, *Skill* was a magazine for weightlifting, bodybuilding and physical culture, and that karate was never mentioned. The magazine has proved untraceable.
20. *Black Belt* magazine – 4 [copies]
21. *Wrestling* magazine – 7 [copies]

22. Film: *Karate Self-Defence* (16 mm.) in wooden travelling case
23. French Championship medallion 1963 – bronze
24. Original Yoseikan Instructional film (Yamaguchi)
25. Film: *The 7th All Japan Karate Championships - June 1963*
26. Envelope containing miscellaneous photographs
27. do.
28. Translation of introductory chapter to Reikichi's book, *Karate-Do*
29. Translation of book by H.D. Plee
30. File containing sundry BKF official photographs
31. Folder containing official photographs for book by H.D. Plee

On Top of Filing Cabinet
1. Yoseikan affiliation certificate of B.K.F. to J.K.A.
2. Fidelity tape recorder with fittings
3. Microphone
4. Lead
5. Book of instructions to be found in drawer in bookcase
6. Portable typewriter Invicta Turino
7. Cine projector Specto 8 mm. (At present at Stratfors Photographic Company, Gants Hill, for repair)

Miscellaneous
1. *Makiwara* (in shed)
2. Sundry B.K.F. rubber stamps (top right-hand drawer of bureau)
3. Key to Upminster *dojo*   (do.   )
4. Black kimono
5. Anatomy atlases – male and female (top left cupboard of book-case)
6. B.K.F. Anatomy Construction Kit
7. Sundry while kimonos
8. Cream Ford 7 cwt. Van, Registration No. 303 WPU Ig. Key FP 642, car key FP 731 – Wilmot Breedins
9. One pair steel expanders
10. One bureau, value £15, personal property of Mr. Bell left to B.K.F., amount to be transferred to private account
11. Large white cupboard containing all B.K.F. circulars, leaflets and stationery
12. Duplicate filing cabinet keys in top right-hand drawer of bureau.'

PART 2

TOTAL BKF APPENDICES (including Eire)[1]

APPENDIX VIII

THE AGE OF BKF KARATEKA AT THE TIME OF THEIR APPLICATION, SPLIT FOR SEX

TABLE 3
THE AGE OF BKF KARATEKA AT THE TIME OF THEIR APPLICATION, SPLIT FOR SEX

	Number	Mean age	SD	Youngest	Oldest	Years covered
BKF (male)	996	24.1	7.1	13	59	1956-1966
BKF (female)	17	21.3	6.4	14	43	1961-1966
BKF (all)	1013	24.1	7.1	13	59	1956-1966

NOTE:

1. See the author's short book, *Shotokan Dawn Over Ireland: A Selected, Early History of Shotokan Karate in Eire (1960-1964),* published by Aiki Pathways, Isle of Man (2006).

The ages of 83.4% of all BKF students are known.

APPENDIX IX

THE MEAN AGE OF BKF KARATEKA AT THE TIME OF THEIR APPLICATION, BY YEAR.

GRAPH 6
A BAR GRAPH SHOWING THE MEAN AGE OF BKF KARATEKA AT THE TIME OF THEIR APPLICATION, BY YEAR.

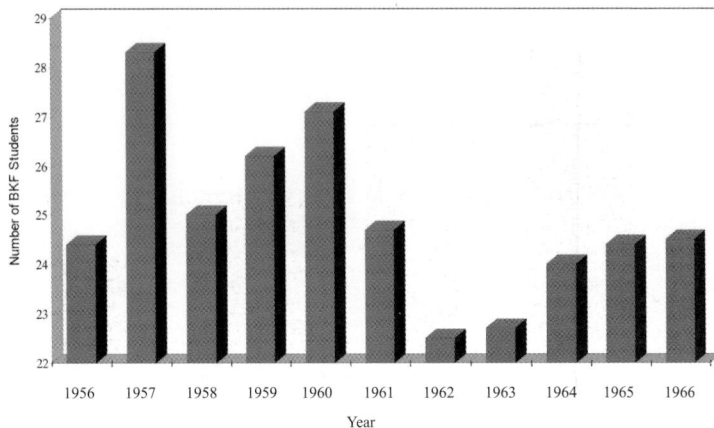

Nō.	5	3	15	20	32	73	87	138	174	257	209
Mean	24.4	28.3	25.0	26.2	27.1	24.7	22.5	22.7	24.0	24.4	24.5
SD	6.4	3.8	6.8	8.3	9.2	6.0	5.9	6.3	7.5	7.3	7.1

Total: 1013

APPENDIX X

THE MEAN AGE OF BKF KARATEKA AT THE TIME OF THEIR APPLICATION, BY LOCATION

GRAPH 7
A BAR GRAPH SHOWING THE MEAN AGE OF BKF KARATEKA AT THE TIME OF THEIR APPLICATION, BY LOCATION

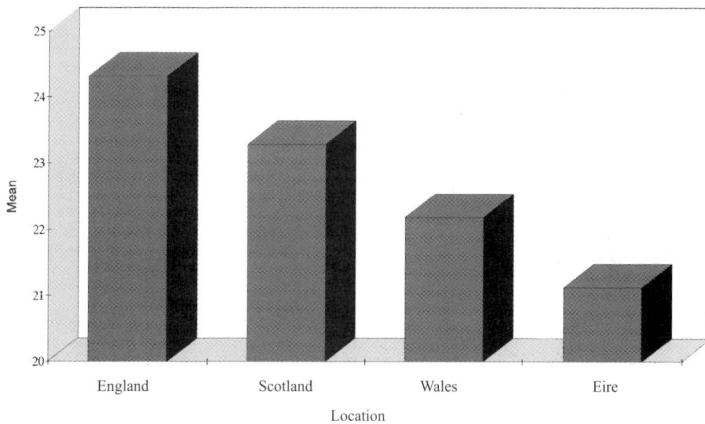

	England	Scotland	Wales	Eire
Nō.	838	114	17	34
Mean	24.3	23.3	22.2	21.1
SD	7.1	6.9	5.2	5.5
Total	1003			

NOTES:

1) If the USAF personnel are treated separately from England (where they practised) then their details, and corrected England details, are:

Location	Nō.	Mean	SD
USAF	28	23.2	5.2
England	810	24.4	7.2

2) Students are included only if their *dojo* is known.

APPENDIX XI

THE SOCIAL CLASS OF BKF KARATEKA AT THE TIME OF THEIR APPLICATION

GRAPH 8
A BAR GRAPH SHOWING THE SOCIAL CLASS OF BKF KARATEKA AT THE TIME OF THEIR APPLICATION

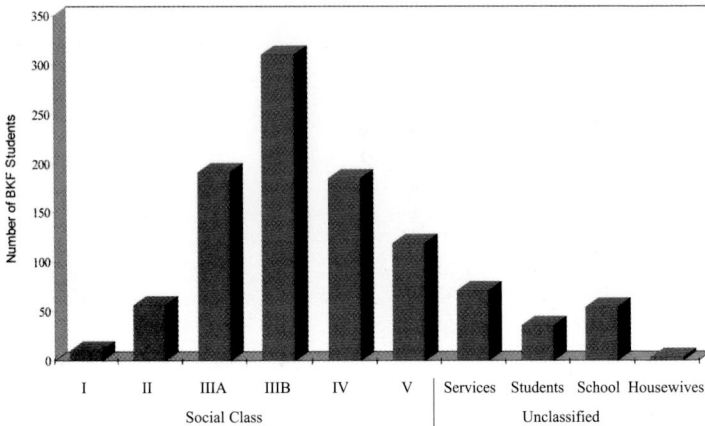

	I	II	IIIA	IIIB	IV	V	Services	Students	School	Housewives
Nō.	10	56	191	310	185	119	71	36	54	3
%	0.97	5.41	18.45	29.95	17.87	11.5	6.86	3.48	5.22	0.29

Total: 1035

NOTE:
1) The social class of 85.3% of all BKF students is known.

APPENDIX XII

THE SOCIAL CLASS OF BKF KARATEKA AT THE TIME OF THEIR APPLICATION, BY YEAR

TABLE 4

THE SOCIAL CLASS OF BKF KARATEKA AT THE TIME OF THEIR APPLICATION, BY YEAR

			SOCIAL CLASS								
	I	II	IIIA	IIIB	IV	V	Services	Student (Unclassified)	School	Housewife	Total
1956	0	1	0	3	2	0	0	0	0	0	6
1957	0	0	3	1	1	2	0	0	0	0	7
1958	0	0	2	5	4	4	1	0	0	0	16
1959	0	1	5	2	4	7	0	1	0	0	20
1960	0	4	10	6	10	5	0	1	2	0	38
1961	1	3	10	16	9	5	25	0	4	0	73
1962	0	1	15	24	18	6	17	1	7	0	89
1963	0	4	16	43	25	13	21	7	8	0	137
1964	2	17	35	58	29	19	0	4	12	0	176
1965	3	9	57	76	49	33	3	10	14	2	256
1966	4	16	38	76	34	25	4	12	7	1	217
Total	10	56	191	310	185	119	71	36	54	3	1035

GRAPH 9
A BAR GRAPH SHOWING THE SOCIAL CLASS OF BKF KARATEKA AT THE TIME OF THEIR APPLICATION, AS A PERCENTAGE BY YEAR

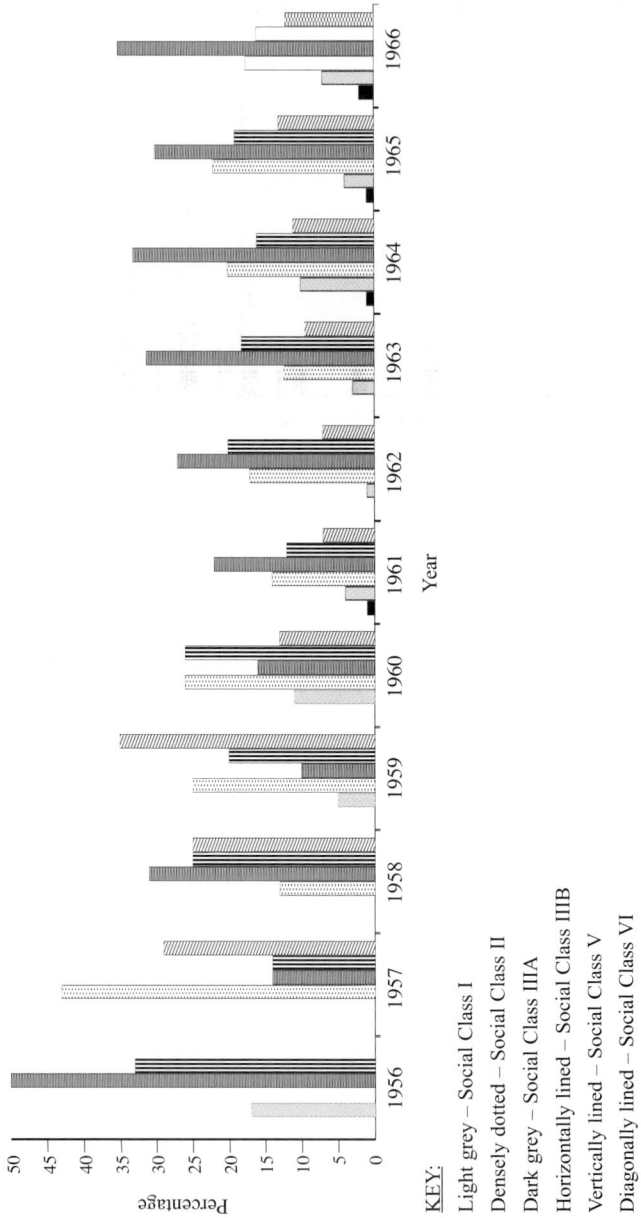

KEY:

Light grey – Social Class I
Densely dotted – Social Class II
Dark grey – Social Class IIIA
Horizontally lined – Social Class IIIB
Vertically lined – Social Class V
Diagonally lined – Social Class VI

GRAPH 10

A BAR GRAPH SHOWING THE DISTRIBUTION OF UNCLASSIFIED BKF
KARATEKA, IN TERMS OF SOCIAL CLASS, AT THE TIME OF THEIR
APPLICATION, AS A PERCENTAGE BY YEAR

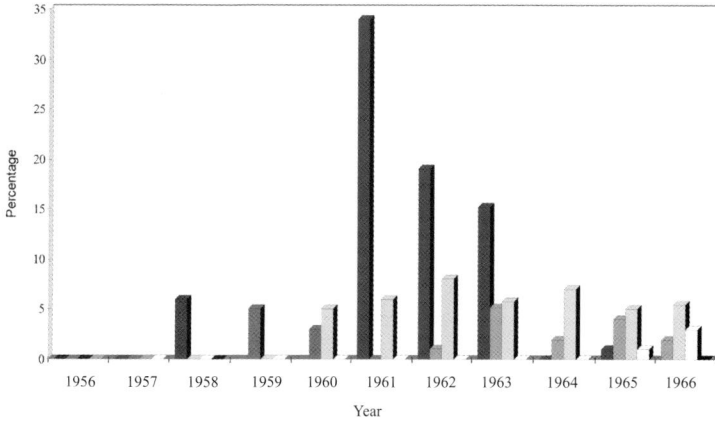

KEY:

Black – Armed Services
Dark grey – Student
Lighty grey – School
White – Housewife

APPENDIX XIII

THE SOCIAL CLASS OF BKF KARATEKA AT THE TIME OF THEIR APPLICATION, BY LOCATION

TABLE 5

THE SOCIAL CLASS OF BKF KARATEKA AT THE TIME OF THEIR APPLICATION, BY YEAR

	SOCIAL CLASS										
	I	II	IIIA	IIIB	IV	V	Services	Student	School (Unclassified)	Housewife	Total
England	9	51	169	247	155	98	69	25	32	3	858
Scotland	1	3	16	45	17	14	0	7	12	0	115
Wales	0	0	1	7	5	1	1	0	2	0	17
Eire	0	1	1	10	7	4	1	4	6	0	34
Total	10	55	187	309	184	117	71	36	52	3	1024

NOTE:

1) Students are included only if their *dojo* is known.

GRAPH 11

A BAR GRAPH SHOWING THE SOCIAL CLASS OF BKF KARATEKA AT THE TIME OF THEIR APPLICATION, AS A PERCENTAGE, BY LOCATION

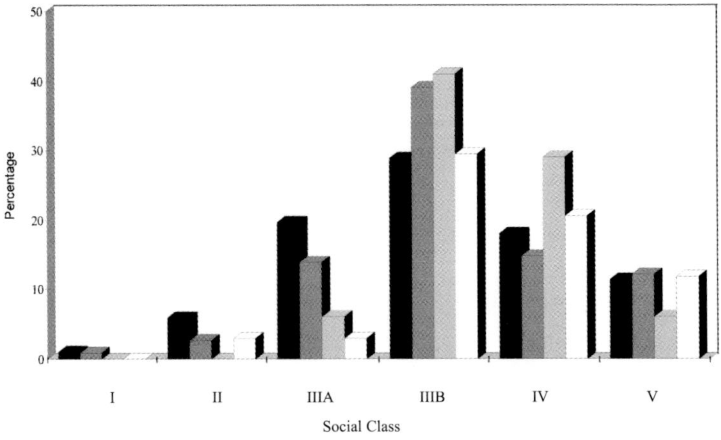

KEY:

Black – England

Dark grey – Scotland

Light grey – Wales

White – Eire

GRAPH 12
A BAR GRAPH SHOWING THE DISTRIBUTION OF UNCLASSIFIED BKF
KARATEKA, IN TERMS OF SOCIAL CLASS, AT THE TIME OF THEIR
APPLICATION, AS A PERCENTAGE, BY LOCATION

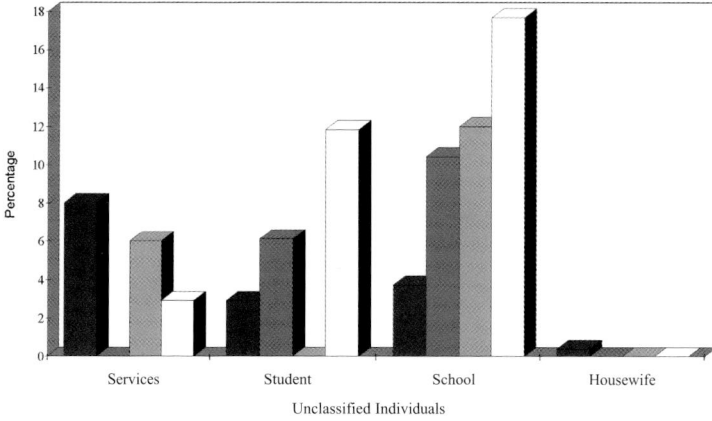

KEY:
Black – England
Dark grey – Scotland
Light grey – Wales
White – Eire

INDEX OF SURNAMES

ABOUT THE AUTHOR

Clive Layton was born in Hertfordshire in 1952, the son of an architect. He began his martial arts training with judo in 1960 under Terry Wingrove, and started Shotokan karate in 1973 under Michael Randall and the Adamou brothers, Nick and Chris, gaining his black belt from Hirokazu Kanazawa in 1977. Originally studying environmental design, he later read for M.A and Ph.D degrees from the University of London, and is a Chartered Psychologist and teacher. Doctor Layton has appeared on both BBC television and radio in connection with his academic work. A prolific writer, with nearly one hundred publications, including twenty books on karate and numerous learned research notes, he has emerged not only as probably the most productive, but, arguably, the finest writer on Shotokan in the world. He has co-authored with famed Okinawan Goju-ryu master, Morio Higaonna; former British manager/coach to the world champion All-Styles karate team, Kyokushinkai master, Steve Arneil; the founder of British karate, Vernon Bell, Michael Randall; and, fellow historian, Harry Cook, amongst others. Doctor Layton's biography, *Kanazawa, 10th Dan*, and, *Funakoshi on Okinawa*, a portrait of life on Okinawa in the 19th century, have recently been published to much acclaim, as has his two volume work, *Shotokan Dawn*, which charts the first ten years of Shotokan karate in Great Britain, and, *Shotokan Dawn Over Ireland*, which gives an account of the establishment of BKF karate in Eire. He has also acted for many years as a consultant reader to the journal, *Perceptual and Motor Skills*, on experimentation into the martial arts. Any spare time is taken up researching new books, pursuing his love of archaeology, genealogy and film, and enjoying the peace of rural life, by the sea, with his wife, daughter and labrador. A highly innovative and deep-thinking *karateka*, he currently holds the rank of 7th Dan.